CHARLES BAUDELAIRE

Paris Spleen

AND

La Fanfarlo

Charles Baudelaire, photographed by Etienne Carjat, c. 1863.

CHARLES BAUDELAIRE

Paris Spleen

AND

La Fanfarlo

*Translated, with Introduction
and Notes, by*

Raymond N. MacKenzie

Hackett Publishing Company, Inc.
Indianapolis/Cambridge

13 12 11 10 09 08   1 2 3 4 5 6 7

For further information, please address
Hackett Publishing Company, Inc.
P.O. Box 44937
Indianapolis, Indiana 46244-0937

www.hackettpublishing.com

Cover design by Abigail Coyle
Interior design and composition by Elizabeth L. Wilson
Printed at Edwards Brothers, Inc.

Library of Congress Cataloging-in-Publication Data

Baudelaire, Charles, 1821–1867.
  [Spleen de Paris. English]
  Paris spleen ; and, La fanfarlo / Charles Baudelaire ; translated, with introduction,
by Raymond N. MacKenzie.
     p. cm.
  ISBN 978-0-87220-948-0 (pbk.) — ISBN 978-0-87220-949-7 (cloth)
  1. Prose poems, French—Translations into English. 2. Paris (France)—Poetry. I.
MacKenzie, Raymond N. II. Baudelaire, Charles, 1821–1867. Fanfarlo. English.
III. Title. IV. Title: Fanfarlo.
  PQ2191.S6E5 2008
  841'.8—dc22

                                                                          2008015340

Contents

Contents

Introduction

Charles Baudelaire is best known as the consummate poet of *The Flowers of Evil* (1857). But superb as those poems are, the reader who knows only them misses an important side of Baudelaire. The novella *La Fanfarlo* (1847) and the prose poems *Paris Spleen* (written between 1857 and 1867, but not published together until 1869, two years after his death), reveal for us the Baudelaire who was intrigued throughout his career by the possibilities of prose. *La Fanfarlo* can be enjoyed simply as a somewhat rambling tale, held together chiefly by its deeply ironic worldview; but coming as it does early in the author's career, it can also be seen as an experiment in fiction, a testing of fiction's limits. The prose poems of *Paris Spleen*, on the other hand, must be ranked among Baudelaire's very greatest achievements: no longer experimental, this highly diverse collection of fifty pieces reveals a writer absolutely sure of exactly what prose can do.

La Fanfarlo: An Experiment in Narrative

La Fanfarlo was probably composed sometime in 1846 and was first published in the January 1847 issue of the *Bulletin de la Société des gens de lettres,* when Baudelaire was twenty-five years old. He had been writing seriously for several years already, and by 1845 he was beginning to have some success in placing a few of his pieces in the booming world of Parisian magazines and newspapers, a world that had been revolutionized by the new phenomenon of the *roman feuilleton,* a serialized novel that appeared on newspapers' front pages. *La Presse,* the paper that inaugurated the front-page fiction section in 1836, had dramatically changed and invigorated French journalism, and had greatly widened the audience for fiction. The *feuilletons* were enormously popular and greatly increased the newspapers' advertising and subscription rates; they paid writers well, and

Baudelaire quickly learned how one must operate to achieve success in this environment: Walter Benjamin noted, for example, that Baudelaire "offered the same manuscript to several papers at the same time and authorized reprints without indicating them as such. From this early period on he viewed the literary market without any illusions."[1] Baudelaire had also already begun what would become his lifelong habit of projecting longer works, many of which were never to be written. A contemporary reader of *La Fanfarlo* would have known the author, if at all, as the promising young art critic who had published intriguing analyses of the art exhibitions the *Salon de 1845* and the *Salon de 1846*.

Indeed, contemporary readers could be forgiven if they saw nothing very groundbreaking in *La Fanfarlo* and regarded it as simply another in the crowd of imitations of Balzac. Baudelaire's story explicitly refers to Balzac's *Girl with the Golden Eyes,* and its plot has much in common with another of Balzac's tales, *Beatrix;* the tone and even the quality of its ironies are reminiscent of other Balzac works, notably *Lost Illusions. La Fanfarlo* also would have had some gossipy resonance for contemporary readers: a story concerning a journalist's love affair with a dancer would inevitably conjure up the memory of Alexandre Henri Dujarier's affair with the scandalous dancer Lola Montez. Dujarier, coeditor of *La Presse,* was shot and killed in a duel in 1845, and when his assailant was tried for murder the following year in Rouen, Montez was the star witness.[2] The papers were full of coverage on the topic, and Baudelaire's story capitalizes on it, as well as on the then-new symbiotic relationship between a star performer and the media. For the contemporary reader, this lurid connection would have been the story's chief interest; indeed, the absence of violence in the dénouement would have been a disappointment. But if the contemporary reader had looked more closely—and had been blessed with the hindsight available to us—

---

1. Walter Benjamin, *Charles Baudelaire: A Lyric Poet in the Era of High Capitalism,* trans. Harry Zohn (London: Verso, 1983), 33. Despite Baudelaire's shrewdness, though, as Benjamin also points out, he made very little profit from his work.

2. The story of Dujarier and Montez is told most fully in Bruce Seymour, *Lola Montez: A Life* (New Haven, CT: Yale University Press, 1996), 70–93.

La Fanfarlo would reveal some extraordinary features that transcend the topical and mark the debut of a restless, searching intelligence.

The plot of the story develops very slowly. The opening pages are primarily a portrait of an inconsequential yet egoistic poet, Samuel Cramer; he is mocked as "the god of impotence" (107) and is so deeply enmeshed in his own delusions of greatness that he responds to genuinely good writing by fantasizing that he wrote it himself. These opening pages seem comic and satiric—and they are—but they are also autobiographical. Nearly every detail in the life of the fictional Cramer is analogous to a detail in the life of Charles Baudelaire.[3] For example, the young Baudelaire had spent his summers in Lyons and had a flirtation or romance with a girl there, which is echoed in the girl whom Samuel Cramer remembers when he meets her again in Paris as Madame de Cosmelly, now a married woman. Cramer's literary tastes and opinions—right down to his attraction to the mysticism of Swedenborg—are those of Baudelaire.[4] Even those details that are not directly autobiographical can be read as a transparent alteration and personalization: Cramer's parents are German and Chilean while Baudelaire's were both French, but behind these fictional nationalities we can glimpse Baudelaire depicting what he saw as the opposed poles of his beloved mother and his loathed stepfather. Claude Pichois directly refers to Cramer as Baudelaire's "double."[5] But Cramer is as often as not

---

3. The connection was noted by Baudelaire's close friend Charles Asselineau, who wrote the poet's first biography in 1869 (*Charles Baudelaire: Sa Vie et son Œuvre*); Asselineau noted that Cramer seems to be an exact self-portrait, right down to the description of his face and hair.

4. Another intriguing connection appears when Baudelaire describes Cramer's narcissistic reading, in which he moves from saying of a book, "this is beautiful enough to have been written by me" to concluding, "therefore, it *is* by me!" Paul Valéry said the same thing about Baudelaire's reaction to Edgar Allan Poe's essay on *The Poetic Principle:* Valéry says, "Baudelaire was so deeply struck by this essay, he received so intense an impression from it, that he considered its contents—and not only the contents but the form itself—*as his own property*" (italics in the original). See Paul Valéry, "The Position of Baudelaire," trans. William Aspenwall Bradley, in *Baudelaire: A Collection of Critical Essays,* ed. Henri Peyre (Englewood Cliffs, NJ: PrenticeHall, 1962), 15.

5. Claude Pichois, *Baudelaire,* trans. Graham Robb (London: Hamish Hamilton, 1989), 144.

depicted as a self-satisfied ass, and thus these opening pages are not only satiric but an exercise in self-analysis so rigorous as to be almost pitiless. Almost—because at some points a certain pride reasserts itself, as when the narrator suddenly corrects us:

> But for all that, don't think that he was incapable of true feelings, and that passion only fluttered lightly across his skin. He would have given the shirt off his back for a man he scarcely knew, a man who, on the basis of his face and his handshake, he had just yesterday decided was his closest friend. In matters of the mind and soul, he showed the lazy contemplation of Germanic natures; in those of passion, his mother's rapid and fickle ardor; and in the practice of life, all the habits of French vanity. He would have got himself wounded in a duel over an author or an artist who had been dead for two centuries. And as he had once been an ardent believer, he later turned passionate atheist. He was at once all the artists he had studied and all the books he had read and yet, despite this thespian faculty, he remained profoundly original. . . . He possessed the logic of all the fine feelings as well as the science of all the low tricks, and yet he never succeeded in any of them because he believed too much in the impossible. Is it any wonder?—For he was always in the process of imagining the impossible. (108–9)

Cramer may, in other words, be absurd enough, and he may have achieved precious little with his literary gifts, but there is a nobility of spirit about him that Baudelaire insists we take seriously.

But *La Fanfarlo* is not only interesting for the self-portrait it includes. Unfolding at a leisurely pace, it is better approached in the spirit of the tale rather than the modern short story (more often tightly unified and swiftly paced), and it has the feeling of an extended anecdote. But it is a highly self-conscious anecdote, and we feel we are in the presence of a narrator who constantly chafes at the elementary necessities of narrative. The long descriptions in the story's early sections, the lengthy disquisitions on novelistic style—these interrupt the plot, or virtually freeze it, and the implication is that the real interest here is not in plot but in practically anything else. The mockery of Cramer—and our awareness that it is also self-mockery—works to subvert the normal expectations we have of a story. At times, the description calls so much attention to itself as description that any illusion of realism is thwarted altogether, as in the moment when Cramer voyeuristically fixates on La Fanfarlo's leg, and the reader expects a sensuous, perhaps erotic, description:

> That leg was already, for Samuel, the object of an infinite desire. Long, thin, stout, and sinewy all at once, it had all the exactitude of the beautiful and all the libertine attraction of the pretty. Sliced perpendicularly at its broadest point, the leg would have formed a kind of triangle whose summit was situated at the tibia, and whose softly rounded calf line would have formed the convex base. (126)

What begins as the erotic becomes so specific and technical as to become ghoulishly comical. Touches like these give Baudelaire's story a kind of *sprezzatura,* an offhandedness that amounts to a defiance of expectations—and they draw attention away from the tale and toward the author. In this sense (among others), Baudelaire never really ceases to be a lyric poet, even when he finds himself needing to be a workaday narrator.

But our expectations are undone again when, in the story's last third, the narrative turns and becomes an efficient, well-paced, highly ironic plot. Cramer is caught in his own trap; the antiwife, the universally desired dancer, turns into the most banal of wives; and the apparently innocent wronged woman, Madame de Cosmelly, turns out to be the greatest winner, and the one who was pulling the strings all along. But this dénouement is not just an exercise in irony, for it calls into question the very nature of desire: Cramer poignantly asks himself toward the end, "Are our passions really sincere? Who can know with certainty what it is that he wants, and accurately read the barometer of his own heart?" (134) The same questions would be taken up half a century later, and would form the core of Marcel Proust's work. Proust knew, as did Baudelaire, that such questions cannot be explored fully and honestly within the confines and conventions of realist fiction; that such questions implicate not only the fictional characters but the author as well. If *La Fanfarlo* does not quite succeed as fiction, the reason is that it is straining to be something else; it is impatient with the exigencies of realist plotting and structure. Fiction, Baudelaire seems to feel here, is insufficient, is overly restrictive, for the kind of psychological and spiritual investigations and self-interrogations that he was driven to attempt. Lyric poetry was more suited to these, but it too would turn out to have its own kinds of limitations. A new form was needed, and Baudelaire found it in the prose poem.

Paris Spleen: The Concept of the Prose Poem

The collection of prose poems known as *Paris Spleen*[6] was published all together only after Baudelaire's death. He planned to continue to add to the collection—as he had done with successive editions of *The Flowers of Evil*—and he projected another fifty titles, which would have doubled the collection's size. The fifty that he completed are, however, entirely finished and polished, and their order is the order Baudelaire intended.

There is a deceptive simplicity to the surface of the fifty poems, a simplicity signaled by the often idiomatic, even offhanded phrasing, along with the abrupt shifts in subject, tone, and setting; almost entirely absent is the formal, even neoclassical grandeur of *The Flowers of Evil,* and in its place is a voice we instantly recognize as the voice of the modern man. Not surprisingly, scholars and critics of Baudelaire have disagreed about even the most fundamental issues regarding *Paris Spleen.* For example, J. A. Hiddleston asserts that the collection reveals "no attempt to group the poems according to theme or 'genre,' or to give the impression of a development or intensification," while Edward K. Kaplan finds in the book an elaborate architecture of doublings and parallels.[7]

---

6. Baudelaire's posthumous editors (Charles Asselineau and Théodore de Banville) gave the collection the title of *Le spleen de Paris,* but this was only one of several possible titles he had envisioned, including *Le rôdeur Parisien* (*The Parisian Prowler*) and, simply, *Petits poèmes en prose.*

7. J. A. Hiddleston, *Baudelaire and "Le Spleen de Paris"* (Oxford: Oxford University Press, 1987), 4; Edward K. Kaplan, *Baudelaire's Prose Poems: The Esthetic, the Ethical, and the Religious in "The Parisian Prowler"* (Athens: University of Georgia Press, 1990).

Some of the difficulty arises from the prefatory letter Baudelaire addresses to Arsène Houssaye (1815–1895), the editor of *La Presse*. We expect a preface to clarify and focus things, but this one raises as many questions as it resolves. First, it is unclear that Baudelaire even wanted to retain the letter as a preface. When first published in *La Presse* on August 26, 1862, it introduced the sequence of the first twenty poems; but later, when Baudelaire drew up his table of contents for the projected book form, he did not include the letter. It is possible, then, that Baudelaire ultimately rejected the letter; it is possible, indeed, that the letter only appeared at all in *La Presse* as a species of flattery to ensure that Houssaye would publish the poems.[8]

Whatever the ultimate intent of the letter, it introduces us to Baudelaire's thinking about the genre of the prose poem:

> Who among us has not dreamed, in his ambitious days, of the miracle of a poetic prose, musical without rhythm or rhyme, supple enough and jarring enough to be adapted to the soul's lyrical movements, to the undulations of reverie, to the twists and turns that consciousness takes? (3)

There would seem to be a very basic contradiction here, as the idea of a prose rhythm that constantly changes and adapts can hardly be said to be a rhythm: rhythm implies a sameness, a pattern of repeated beats. But Baudelaire is in search of a rhythm without formalized repetition, a rhythm that changes as continually as life and our human consciousness does. How radical this is can be shown when we see the reductio ad absurdum that it seems to invite: we would know the prose poet has succeeded if he has entirely avoided what we normally call rhythm; the prose poem is a poem that avoids the defining characteristic of poetry. How can we address this apparent paradox—how can we see the pieces in *Paris Spleen* as *poems*?

8. Kaplan reads the letter as a kind of mockery of Houssaye disguised as flattery (see *Baudelaire's Prose Poems*, 9–12). This may be overly subtle, however. There is no doubt that Baudelaire, in some moods, despised Houssaye for his power and his success in the literary world, and there is no doubt that Baudelaire saw himself as by far the greater talent. But to mock Houssaye within the pages of his own paper would seem to be playing a dangerous game.

Anne Jamison has recently explored what she calls Baudelaire's "aesthetics of transgression,"[9] his insistence that art must surprise and even shock, that it must break free from restraints that inevitably deaden it. She cites a passage from one of his essays on Poe concerning poetic rhythm:

> There is one point in which the story is superior even to the poem. Rhythm is necessary to the development of the idea of beauty, which is the noblest aim of the poet. Now, the artifices of rhythm form an insurmountable obstacle to that painstaking development of thoughts and expressions that have *truth* as their goal.[10]

Jamison argues that the prose poem is a deliberately transgressive genre, one that breaks with our conventional expectations of "pure" prose or poetry, a genre "perpetually generating strangeness by violating what had elsewhere been defined as pure."[11] Neither poetry as such nor the conventional uses of prose are adequate to "the soul's lyrical movements, to the undulations of reverie, to the twists and turns that consciousness takes." But prose offers the writer some flexibilities unavailable to the poet, as Baudelaire went on to note in the same essay:

> Moreover, the author of a story has available to him a multitude of tones, of nuances in language, tones of reasoning, of sarcasm, of humor, all of which poetry repudiates, and which are kinds of dissonance, of outrages upon the idea of pure beauty.

Baudelaire is attracted to prose because of the expanded palette it offers, a repertoire of possibilities for going beyond the classical (or

---

9. Anne Jamison, "Any Where Out of this Verse: Baudelaire's Prose Poetics and the Aesthetics of Transgression," *Nineteenth-Century French Studies* 29 (Spring–Summer 2001), 280.

10. Baudelaire, "Notes nouvelles sur Edgar Poe" [1857], in *Œuvres Complètes,* ed. Claude Pichois (Paris: Gallimard, 1976), 2: 329–30 (later citations of this text will be abbreviated OC).

11. Jamison, "Any Where Out of this Verse," 280.

the romantic) idea of beauty, for forging a suitable response to the world as it is, not the world as idealized in traditional art and poetry. Reasoning, or thinking through what the world presents to us, responding to it with sarcasm, finding comedy in it: this is the realm of spleen, of that restless dissatisfaction, sometimes irritable or melancholic, sometimes ribald and hilarious, but always unsettled, always shifting and recoiling at each new and unforeseen experience.

Baudelaire's impulse here may sound very much like a typical nineteenth-century one, akin to the impulse toward Realism, which often implied a refusal of form, or at least of classical form. Realism, too, resulted from a search for a means of depicting hitherto excluded aspects of experience, aspects that had traditionally been regarded as unworthy of the artist's attention. And it is more than coincidence that the mid-nineteenth century gave rise not only to Realism in art and fiction but also to the new technology of the photograph: photography can capture the moment exactly as it is without imposing a preexisting form, which would only falsify the moment. Baudelaire, though, was ambivalent about Realism, and despite his friendship with the great Félix Nadar, he inveighed bitterly against the public taste for photography in his *Salon de 1859*, seeing it as the modern age's vengeance upon art and the imagination, a glorification of the merely material. The prose poem for Baudelaire was not simply an opportunity to create what we would call Realist literature, and it is decidedly not a rejection of the poetic in favor of prose fiction. His rejection of formal poetic rhythm is not a rejection of the poetic or the lyrical in the wider senses of those terms. He does not want to give up on the idea of rhythm altogether—only on the limitations, the boundary-setting, that repetition involves. He wants to achieve what we might call a momentary or provisional rhythm, the always new and different rhythm that arises from the shock and suddenness of modern urban life—the suddenness of turning a corner, or encountering a crowd, or seeing a stranger we suddenly realize we have met before. Or, as he puts it in his preface to Houssaye:

> My obsession with this ideal was born primarily out of frequenting vast cities, out of the intersections of their infinite connections. (4)

The Baudelairean prose poem, then, is in its essence an urban phenomenon, born out of the encounter with the sheer complexity and diversity of the great modern city.

Photography as an analogy does not apply to *Paris Spleen*, for in these poems we enter not so much into the sheer material realities of Paris as into the mediating consciousness of the poet—his fantasies, his reflections, his recollections of experience, often in sharply fragmentary form. As an inspiration, he invokes Aloysius Bertrand's (1807–1841) short collection *Gaspard of the Night: Fantasies in the Manner of Rembrandt and Callot,* set in medieval Dijon: while reading Bertrand, he writes to Houssaye,

> the idea came to me to try something similar, to apply the method he used to depict ancient life, so strangely picturesque, to modern life, or rather to *a* modern and more abstract life. (3)

The distinction here is crucial: *Paris Spleen* is not a book about modern life but about *a* modern life: the consciousness of the individual poet/narrator is essential to it, not simply a filter through which we see Paris life. Yet the book is not to be simply the record of an individual's perceptions, and certainly not to be simply autobiographical. It is the record of "a modern and more abstract life," more abstract than what we expect from conventional first-person narration, and far more fluid and open. The modern life, the modern self, is indeed more fluid and open, more varied, sometimes dizzyingly so, and this is the life Baudelaire wishes to get at, a subject best approached through the prose poem.

A powerful example of this is "At One in the Morning," number 10 in the collection. It appears to be almost a diary entry, an explicit rundown of the day's events; those events seem to be precisely the kind that Charles Baudelaire would have experienced in the hectic and hypocritical world of the literary marketplace of his day. But the hypocrisy the narrator sees in others is also present in himself; while he wants to condemn the others, and wants to escape to the freedom and integrity of solitude, he nonetheless implicates himself in the world of hypocrisy and baseness. As Sonya Stephens puts it, his individual self—the self he urgently wants to protect and separate from the vile others—becomes "blurred . . . by a hypocrisy and perverseness which progressively undermine the difference between the self and others"; in pieces like this one, she continues,

> The "I" is an indecipherable mix of autobiography and fiction, referring simultaneously and indissociably both to a historical, biographical figure, to the poet as person, and to a figure that is entirely constructed, or fictive—a figure of the poet become character in an allegorical fiction of poetic creativity.[12]

This is, at least in part, what Baudelaire seems to mean by "a modern and more abstract life."

The preface dedicated to Houssaye, then, opens up for us a number of avenues for appreciating what Baudelaire's aims were for the prose poems, though it is by no means a definitive or complete theory of the genre. Edward K. Kaplan has suggested that a more satisfactory theory is to be found in "The Thyrsus," number 32 in the collection. In this piece, addressed to Franz Liszt, Baudelaire finds a powerfully suggestive emblem in the ancient thyrsus—a staff around which vines were wound. The thyrsus was used in ancient Greece by priests and followers of Dionysus (it figures prominently, for example, in Euripides' *The Bacchae*); it carries with it connotations of unleashed sexuality and violence, of the profound power of the irrational, but it is in itself a thing of duality, as Baudelaire emphasizes:

> What is a thyrsus? In the moral and poetic sense, it is a sacerdotal emblem held in the hands of priests or priestesses celebrating the divinity of whom they are the interpreters and servants. But physically it's only a stick, just a stick, like the ones used for supporting vines, dry, stiff, and straight. Around the stick are wound stems and flowers that seem to meander capriciously, playing, frolicking, some sinuous and fugitive, some hanging down like bells or upside-down cups. And a stunning glory springs from this complexity of line and color,

---

12. Sonya Stephens, "Contingencies and Discontinuities of the Lyric I: Baudelaire as Poet-Narrator and Diarist," in *Baudelaire and the Poetics of Modernity*, ed. Patricia A. Ward (Nashville, TN: Vanderbilt University Press, 2001), 140–41.

sometimes tender, sometimes bold. Doesn't it seem as if the curved line and the spiral are paying court to the straight line, dancing around it in mute adoration? Doesn't it seem as if all these delicate corollas, all these calyxes, exploding with scent and color, are performing a mystical fandango around the hieratic stick? (71)

The thyrsus, Baudelaire continues, is thus a suitable emblem for the power of Liszt's music—and by natural extension, for art in general, especially the art of *Paris Spleen*. As Kaplan puts it, "Baudelaire stresses the *combination* of 'prosaic' and 'poetic' elements, the interweaving of shapes, colors, and scents, which exercises a mysterious seduction."[13]

The artist then, Liszt or Baudelaire, musician or poet, is a creator of amalgamations, of new combinations of experience. Put this way, Baudelaire's "The Thyrsus" seems to anticipate T. S. Eliot's famous formulation:

When a poet's mind is perfectly equipped for its work, it is constantly amalgamating disparate experience; the ordinary man's experience is chaotic, irregular, fragmentary.[14]

Invoking Eliot is perhaps another way of saying that *Paris Spleen* can be seen as the inaugural text of what we have come to call Modernism.

Baudelaire and the Moral Response

Charles Baudelaire is like Nietzsche in at least one respect: it is possible to quote him to support utterly contradictory views. He can be quoted to sound like a Satanist, a blasphemer, an atheist; and he can also be quoted to appear like a deeply conservative Catholic (which is how he was read by Barbey D'Aurevilly, Léon Bloy, and François Mauriac). He can sound like a raging misogynist, and he can also

13. Kaplan, *Baudelaire's Prose Poems*, 13.

14. T. S. Eliot, "The Metaphysical Poets" [1921], in *Selected Prose of T. S. Eliot*, ed. Frank Kermode (New York: Harcourt Brace Jovanovich, 1975), 64.

speak tenderly and sympathetically of women. And when he turns to the subject of writing, he can proclaim the ultimate end of art to be the production of beauty and its ultimate bane to be morality. Yet he can, as we have seen, seek out a literary form that will let him perform "outrages" upon beauty. Perhaps most striking, though, is how this self-proclaimed aesthete can, especially in *Paris Spleen,* write a book that is one of the most morally incisive of anything produced in the century. This collection of prose poems functions as an interrogation of conventional morality, and it also reveals an always honest, sometimes anguished quest for an appropriate ethical response to experience and to others.

The concern with the ethical in the modern world is implicit in the very opening piece, "The Foreigner." This seemingly simple dialogue poses two problems for the English translator. First is the title: while the French *étranger* can be either "foreigner" or "stranger," I have chosen the former to emphasize the respondent's uprootedness and homelessness, contrasted so vividly with his interlocutor's comfortable situation. Second is the French distinction between *vous* and *tu.* The interlocutor poses his questions in the informal (or intimate, or condescending) *tu* form, while the foreigner responds with the formal (or respectful, or deliberately distancing) *vous* form—a distinction not available in English, but crucial because it anchors the two speakers in utterly different social realms and implies a power differential between the two. The questioner is at home in every sense, rooted in his materialistic comfort (he loves gold and detests God), and seems mildly puzzled at the phenomenon of this Other who clearly does not belong there; and when the dialogue is over, he is probably no less puzzled. The two speakers will never understand each other. Julia Kristeva, speaking of literal foreigners and immigrants (and we should be careful not to literalize the respondent's foreignness), seems to be describing the metaphysical status of Baudelaire's "foreigner":

> Free of ties with his own people, the foreigner feels "completely free." Nevertheless, the consummate name of such a freedom is solitude. Useless or limitless, it amounts to boredom or supreme availability. . . . Available, freed of everything, the

foreigner has nothing, he is nothing. But he is ready for the absolute, if an absolute could choose him.[15]

The "absolute" attracting Baudelaire's character is figured in the last line, the answer to what it is he loves: "the clouds passing . . . up there, up there . . . the marvelous clouds." Reading this concluding line for the first time, we might feel we are on familiar ground at last: the respondent, the "foreigner," is the poet with his "head in the clouds," as we would say, an idealist rejecting the comforts of the material, which is represented here by the comfortable questioner. We might feel that we are in the realm of conventional Romanticism. But there is an important, non- or post-Romantic tonality in the representation of the poet and the world he seems to reject. First, there is no trace of self-pity, no expression of *weltschmerz,* but on the contrary we sense pride and even defiance: he says he hates gold "as you hate God" (5). His use of the formal *vous* is not deference—though the questioner might want to see it that way—but instead it signals a firm distancing and an utter self-possession.

What of the clouds? Should we read them as distant hints of an absolute, of a transcendent realm, and as markers of God's presence? Or should we read his love of them as being based simply on their being "up there" and passing, as markers, instead, of sheer transience? Are they loved because they are so distant and ephemeral, symbols of almost nonbeing? Clouds are prominent in a number of other pieces in *Paris Spleen,* two of which are especially relevant. The first is in "Vocations," number 31 in the collection. There, one of the four boys in the park is convinced he sees God in the evening clouds:

> One of the four children, who for some time had no longer been listening to his comrade's discourse, watching some distant spot in the sky with a strange fixity, suddenly said: "Look, look up there! Do you see that? He's sitting on that little isolated cloud, that fire-colored cloud moving so slowly. Him too, it's as if He's watching us."

15. Julia Kristeva, *Strangers to Ourselves,* trans. Leon S. Roudiez (New York: Columbia University Press, 1991), 12.

"Who? Who is it?" the others asked.

"God!" he said in a perfectly convinced voice. "Oh! He's already far away; soon you won't be able to see Him. He must be traveling, on His way to visit all the other countries. Wait, He's going to pass beyond that row of trees that's almost at the horizon . . . and now He's sinking behind the church tower . . . Ah, you can't see Him anymore!" And the child stayed turned in that direction for a long time, his eyes fixed on the line separating earth and sky, shining with an ineffable expression of ecstasy and regret. (67)

Though the child's vision is dismissed by the others as "crazy," we are nevertheless invited to superimpose this cloud vision on the one in "The Foreigner," and perhaps to see a connection between the foreigner and the visionary boy.

But another cloud instance complicates that superimposition: poem number 44, "The Soup and the Clouds," is another brief and apparently simple piece:

My beloved little maniac was making me dinner, and from the open window of the dining room I contemplated the drifting architectures that God makes out of vapors, those marvelous constructions of the impalpable. And in my contemplation, I was saying to myself: "All these phantasmal clouds are almost as beautiful as the eyes of my beautiful beloved, my darling monstrous little green-eyed maniac."

And suddenly I felt a violent punch in my back, and I heard a husky, charming voice, a hysterical voice hoarsened by brandy, the voice of my dear little beloved, who was saying: "So are you going to eat your soup, you son of a bitch of a cloud merchant?" (89)

The structural parallel between this and "The Foreigner" is striking: the cloud-obsessed poet's encounter with a vigorously materialist interlocutor. "The Soup and the Clouds" seems to function as self-mockery, like the self-mockery of *La Fanfarlo*, as an anecdote of self-deflation. But, again, there is something much richer and more complex at work here. Kara M. Rabbitt offers a stimulating reading of the poem, seeing in it "a triangulation of interpretation" that recurs frequently in the collection. In this triangulation,

> the speaking subject's view of an other is challenged by the voice of another, often but not always by that same other serving instead as an interlocutor. These moments frequently occur just as the interpreting subject is using the other—his beloved, a friend, or a stranger—as an idealized mirror in which he reads that which he would want to see as self.[16]

Rabbitt calls attention here to what I would argue is central to *Paris Spleen,* the quest for a true view of the world—of self and other— that would enable us to form an adequate, honest, lucid moral response. Partial views, especially egocentric ones, get corrected by the intrusion of the Other, a movement that is sometimes comic, as in "The Soup and the Clouds." (This same movement informs another great post-Romantic work, Byron's *Don Juan;* a comparison of that work with *Paris Spleen* could be very worthwhile.) I would argue further that this corrective movement occurs not only within many of the individual prose poems but also across the whole collection—that later pieces deepen, complicate, enrich, and correct earlier ones.

In saying this, of course, I am contradicting a point Baudelaire himself makes in the dedication to Houssaye:

> My dear friend, I send you here a little work of which no one could say that it has neither head nor tail, because, on the contrary, everything in it is both head and tail, alternately and reciprocally. Please consider what fine advantages this combination offers to all of us, to you, to me, and to the reader. We can cut wherever we like—me, my reverie, you, the manuscript, and the reader, his reading; for I don't tie the impatient reader up in the endless thread of a superfluous plot. Pull out one of the vertebrae, and the two halves of this tortuous fantasy

---

16. Kara M. Rabbitt, "Reading and Otherness: The Interpretative Triangle in Baudelaire's *Petits poèmes en prose," Nineteenth-Century French Studies* 33, 3–4 (Spring–Summer 2005), 358.

will rejoin themselves painlessly. Chop it up into numerous fragments, and you'll find that each one can live on its own. (3)

Of course, *Paris Spleen* can be read in this way; the reader can, and in some respects must, approach each prose poem on its own terms. And certainly Baudelaire emphatically strove to avoid any continuous narrative; the book instead seems to give the impression of randomness or "givenness." Yet reading the collection as a whole, one is struck by a moral progression, a slowly deepening and focusing viewpoint on the wildly diverse world depicted in its fifty pieces.

The moral question, at its simplest, is how one ought to live, how one ought to respond to experience, to the Other who looms into view at every street corner. The morality that evolves in *Paris Spleen* is emphatically not dogmatic, or rigid, or preconceived; it is not a system of rules that are imposed upon experience, not a list of do's and don'ts that readily lead to judgment or condemnation of the Other who fails to conform to them. The world of experience—the world of characters and incidents in *Paris Spleen*—is a world of constant shifts and twists and shocks; what is needed if one wants to live honestly in such a world is not only a literary *form* supple enough to accommodate those shocks, but a morality or ethics just as supple, just as open to the new and the unexpected. The problem with "conventional morality," in other words, is that it is conventional, that it inevitably leads to a dishonest response, that it eventually reveals itself to be closed to experience. Perhaps the most striking feature of the morality of Baudelaire's book is the way in which it evolves, the way in which it responds rather than predetermines.

The next few prose poems in the collection illustrate the point. The second poem, "The Old Woman's Despair," invites us to feel pity for the rejected old woman who only wants to please and love the child; and the fourth poem, "A Joker," invites us to feel "rage" at the unfeeling wit who mocks the hardworking donkey. The fourth poem seems to replay and recast the second one, to deepen our own response to these two very different yet somehow similar instances of rejection, these two failures of moral response. In "A Joker," the poet himself speaks his rage and generalizes it: the joker "seemed to me the incarnation of the very soul of France" (8). Just as the infant could not see the inner reality, the love in the old woman, so the joker cannot see the pathos and nobility of the humble, "zealous" donkey. And the generalization about the "soul of France" tells us that this lack of moral insight is a social norm in the modern world. Just as these two poems comment on each other, they both add a dimension to the opening poem: is the figure of the joker implicit in the smug questioner of "The Foreigner" with his condescending *tu*? These early poems in *Paris Spleen* announce a sympathy with the rejected, the ugly, the contemptible; it is, therefore, easy to see why radical Christians like Léon Bloy counted Baudelaire as one of their own.[17]

But the morality of *Paris Spleen* is not simply that of a Christian sympathy for the despised and rejected, for between the despiser and the despised there is a third figure: the artist, who is foregrounded in the third poem, "The Artist's Confiteor." The artist appears between the pieces about the old woman and the joker to remind us that we only know about them through the artist's mediation. The Romantic poet likewise foregrounds the artist, but for the Romantic, the artist is elevated to a figure of moral authority. The point is clear if we contrast Baudelaire's "A Joker" with a poem of similar content, Coleridge's "To a Young Ass," which begins, "Poor little foal of an oppressed Race! / I love the languid Patience of thy face . . ."[18] Baudelaire does not announce his "love" of the donkey, nor even dwell on its "oppressed" nature, but instead implies respect for its humble work before turning to rage at the fool who mocks it. There is a world of difference with Coleridge's speaker, who demonstrates his own sensibility, his own moral authority at once. Baudelaire's "The Artist's Confiteor" questions that authority. A confiteor is a formal confession of sins, and by locating this poem at precisely this point in the collection, Baudelaire shows that the artist's point of view—his own point of view—will likewise be subject to interrogation. The moral certainty of a Coleridge or

17. It is worth recalling that the donkey has always been closely associated with Christ in Christian art: see Thomas F. Mathews, *The Clash of Gods: A Reinterpretation of Christian Art* (Princeton, NJ: Princeton University Press, 1993), especially chapter 2.

18. Samuel Taylor Coleridge, "To a Young Ass," in *Samuel Taylor Coleridge*, ed. H. J. Jackson (Oxford: Oxford University Press, 1985), 10.

Wordsworth, of a Chateaubriand or a Lamartine, will sometimes be seen in *Paris Spleen,* but just as often it will evaporate in self-interrogation, self-doubt, even self-loathing.

"The Artist's Confiteor" is a confession of the sin of pride: the artist's "rival" is Nature itself, a rival who, when raising him up to the level of the infinite, sometimes seems an accomplice, but who then turns and presents itself as an impenetrable wall between the artist and the infinite. And Nature always wins; the poet's colossal ego is always deflated—or, rather, the smallness of the ego is always reestablished. If, for a moment, "in the grandeur of reverie, the 'me' is quickly lost" (7), that loss is never permanent; the finite, with its sick nerves, returns to obliterate the moment. Or, to use the language of "The Foreigner," the marvelous clouds always remain "up there."

The post-Romantic artist remains a seeker of the infinite, but this search now seems more a compulsion, a neurosis, rather than a sign of superiority; the search for the infinite is a perpetually recurring defeat, and it suggests that the moral authority in pieces like "The Old Woman's Despair" and "A Joker" is best seen as provisional. Thus, "The Artist's Confiteor" functions as a corrective, a caution as we learn how to read *Paris Spleen* that we must keep our own interpretations and responses provisional as well. Moreover, in being effectively rejected by the infinite, the artist is classed with the old woman and the humble donkey; the artist too is rejected.

The presence of the artist so early in *Paris Spleen* is not a species of Romantic self-dramatization, like that of Samuel Cramer's in his *Ospreys* volume, but of self-interrogation and even confession. The moral question of how to live becomes an epistemological question: given my uncertain vision, how can I know the truth about what I see? Truth, like the absolute, like the infinite, does seem to exist; like the passing clouds "up there," we seem to be given glimpses of it, of another, truer world. Throughout his works, Baudelaire frequently describes the world as a system of mysterious signs, as a kind of allegory. Thus, in an unfinished sketch on the subject of Realism, he notes:

> Poetry is what we have of what is most real, it is what is com-
> pletely true only in another world.—This world here,—a dic-
> tionary of hieroglyphics.[19]

And in the *Salon de 1859*, he states that the fundamental principle
of aesthetics is this allegorical vision:

> The entire visible universe is only a storehouse of images and
> signs to which the imagination accords relative place and
> importance; it is like food for the imagination to digest and
> transform.[20]

And in 1861, in an essay on Victor Hugo, he writes that if we
observe carefully, we will inevitably arrive at this truth:

> . . . everything is hieroglyphic, and we know that symbols are
> only obscure in a relative sense, that is, relative to the purity,
> the good will, or the native insight of our souls. Now what is
> a poet (I use the term in its widest sense) if he is not a transla-
> tor, a decipherer?[21]

This sense that the world is a system of signs to be decoded, that
meaning awaits us everywhere, and that the poet is the great reader
and "translator" of that vast other language ("allegory" originally
meant "other speech")—all this seems to amount to a statement of
faith and to a profound optimism. For example, Baudelaire's theory
of allegory seems to place him on the side of his English contempo-
rary Robert Browning, who makes one of his characters say, "This
world's no blot for us, / Nor blank; it means intensely, and means
good: / To find its meaning is my meat and drink."[22] And yet a
Browning-like optimism is one of the last traits we would normally

---

19. Baudelaire, "Puisque réalisme il y a" [1855], OC 2: 59.

20. Baudelaire, *Salon de 1859,* OC 2: 627.

21. Baudelaire, "Victor Hugo," in *Réflexions sur quelques-uns de mes contemporains,*
OC 2: 133.

22. Robert Browning, "Fra Lippo Lippi" [1855], in *Robert Browning,* ed. Adam
Roberts (Oxford: Oxford University Press, 1997), ll. 313–15, 181.

ascribe to Baudelaire, whose work so often takes us into the soul's darkest places—as in "At One in the Morning" (number 10), for instance, or "Any Where Out of the World" (number 48).

In fact, the tension between the sense of allegory—that there is meaning, that the world is composed of signs that try to speak to us—and the sense of despair at the world's casual horror is at the heart of *Paris Spleen*. The figure of the artist dominates the book, especially the figure of the artist as seeking, momentarily achieving, and then again losing his grip on the world he tries to "decipher." One of Baudelaire's most sensitive and influential readers was Walter Benjamin, who returned often in his work to the difficulties of Baudelairean allegory.[23] For Benjamin, Baudelaire is the essential figure of the modern artist adrift in a world of metaphysical "ruin," and his spleen—his rage, frustration, despair—both result from and help reveal a world where meaning and appearance have parted company. Thus, instead of the artist as sage, with a serene, comprehensive view of life, we have a poet experiencing "the twists and turns that conscience takes," born out of the experience of modern cities and "the intersections of their infinite connections" (4).

The quest for a responsive and responsible ethics is greatly complicated by the brokenness of meaning, the indeterminacy of the allegory, and the weaknesses of the artist himself, the "decipherer." Some of the prose poems in *Paris Spleen* seem to gesture at a clearer, more parable-like allegory. "Cake" (number 15), for example, seems a grimly comic view of the inherently "fratricidal" aspect of human nature—or perhaps it suggests the bestial level to which material want reduces us. "The Toy of the Poor" (number 19) seems to echo faintly the situation of "Cake," with the poor child and the rich one grinning at each other at the sight of the caged rat—though here, too, the ironies are complex, as the rich child is also "caged" behind the gate of his chateau. How are we to understand the "fraternity" of these two children? Equally problematic is the allegory of "Beautiful

---

23. Benjamin's writings on Baudelaire are collected in *The Writer on Modern Life: Essays on Charles Baudelaire* (Cambridge, MA: Harvard University Press, 2006). A helpful summary of Benjamin's theory of Baudelairean—and hence modern—allegory may be found in Theresa M. Kelley, *Reinventing Allegory* (Cambridge: Cambridge University Press, 1997), 251–62.

Dorothy" (number 25). This poem, one of a number that take us out of the Western, urban world, is a highly visual, almost painterly depiction of the ex-slave Dorothy who now works as a prostitute, saving her earnings to buy her sister's freedom. In such a situation, we have to ask what "freedom" means, and we see commerce—which for Baudelaire entails the commodification of the human person—at the root of all human relations, and certainly at the root of the attraction the Europeans, Dorothy's clients, feel for her. As one recent analysis puts it, the poem

> is seemingly an allegory of the social and economic processes that have entered the realm of art and literature, thereby necessitating a break with the Romantic idealization of nature and feminine beauty.[24]

The "economic processes" of modern capitalism and their debilitating effects on the person—and also on the artist and his art—fuel many of the poems of *Paris Spleen* and comprise another of the impediments to the quest for a moral stance.

A conventionally sympathetic response to social and economic problems—of indignation, of declaring the bourgeois artist's solidarity with the poor and calling for reforms to address socioeconomic inequities—such a response is not available to Baudelaire, or at least not in an uncomplicated form. In this respect, it is instructive to consider Baudelaire's reaction to Victor Hugo's *Les Misérables,* perhaps the greatest example of a novel that enjoins upon the reader a deep sympathy for the poor. Baudelaire reviewed the novel, giving it what seemed to be the highest possible praise—certainly the kind of praise calculated to flatter Hugo, who was then the most famous writer in France. In his review, Baudelaire wrote:

> This book is a book of charity, that is, a book created to stimulate, to provoke the spirit of charity; it is a questioning book, posing socially complex cases of a terrible, overwhelming

---

24. Jennifer Forest and Catherine Jaffe, "Figuring Modernity: Juan Ramon Jimenez and the Baudelairean Tradition of the Prose Poem," *Comparative Literature* 48, 3 (Summer 1996), 274.

nature, saying to the reader's conscience: "Well then! What do you think? What do you conclude?"[25]

The review seems to recognize and praise Hugo's intention, execution, and effect. But Claude Pichois points out that Baudelaire said something very different in private, speaking to his friend Asselineau:

> "Ah!" he said angrily, "what is it with these sentimental criminals who feel remorse over a matter of forty sous, who debate for hours with their consciences . . . ? . . . Me, I'll write a novel that introduces a villain, but a real villain, an assassin, thief, arsonist and bandit, that concludes with this statement: 'And beneath the shade of these trees I have planted, surrounded by a family that venerates me, children who love me and a wife who adores me—I enjoy in peace the fruits of my crimes.'"[26]

We can accuse Baudelaire of hypocrisy in his published review, but if we do, we would have to indict virtually every writer in the literary marketplace. More to the point, in his private response what he detests is the sentimentalizing of reality in Hugo's novel. Truth is more valuable than fine feelings. While a novelist like Hugo might have insisted on our pity for the ex-slave Dorothy, for example, Baudelaire presents her as she is without imposing a reaction on us. And while Baudelaire can express disgust and even rage against those who fail to sympathize—as he does in "A Joker" (number 4) or "The Eyes of the Poor" (number 26)—we always understand that we are observing disgust or rage, not being manipulated into feeling it ourselves.

Baudelaire, like his great contemporary Flaubert, felt a deep loathing for cliché, including clichéd moral responses. And perhaps paradoxically, this loathing, present throughout *Paris Spleen,* will end up giving the book a real moral authority—real because earned. The book presents us with some outrageous moments, which are calculated to undermine any traditional moral authority—the attack

---

25. Baudelaire, review of *Les Misérables* [1862], OC 2: 220.

26. Quoted in OC 2: 1182.

on the poor old glazier in "The Bad Glazier" (number 9) is a memorable example, as is the wildly over the top "Let's Beat Up the Poor!" (number 49), where the narrator's gratuitous assault on the old beggar is offered to us in gleeful detail. But both of these poems are built upon multiple ironies, and it would be a blind reader indeed who took them for immoral poems. (The most delightful irony in the latter poem is that attacking a beggar with a tree branch is treating him with more respect as a human being than he gets from all the vacuous social theorists.) Baudelaire refuses the cheap, easy moral high ground in pieces like these, and in a number of other poems he makes a point of implicating himself in human weaknesses and sins (such as in numbers 21 and 29, "The Temptations: Or Eros, Plutus, and Fame" and "The Generous Gambler").

But nowhere is this self-implication more naked and honest, nowhere is it less satiric or ironic, than in the powerful "At One in the Morning" (number 10). After a recitation of his day's activities, marked by humiliation and hypocrisy and weakness, he concludes with what we must take as a genuine, heartfelt prayer:

> Souls of those I have loved, souls of those I have sung, strengthen me, support me, distance me from the lie and the corrupting vapors of the world, and you, my Lord God! Give me the grace to produce a few beautiful lines to prove to myself that I am not the least of men, that I am not inferior to those whom I despise! (19)

This is a variation—a very significant variation—on the famous prayer of the Pharisee: "I thank you, Lord, that I am not made like other men" (Luke 18:1–14). Unlike the Pharisee reveling in his superiority, Baudelaire is only too aware that he *is* made like all the others.

There are other instances of prayer in *Paris Spleen*, but one in particular seems climactic, as it in important ways deepens and extends the prayer of "At One in the Morning." This is the prayer that appears at the end of "Mademoiselle Bistouri" (number 47), and both the poem and the prayer form the moral and spiritual core of *Paris Spleen*. By this point in the collection we have seen many instances of perversity, but none of them has overwhelmed the narrator until now. Mademoiselle Bistouri's "collecting" of surgeons, her sexual fetish for blood on their smocks—all this is gruesome enough, and the narrator responds at first with contempt and even ridicule. But he slowly gives in to an almost clinical fascination with her as a "case" to be analyzed; he responds, in other words, in a detached, technical, amoral manner (much like the doctor he denies being). Or perhaps we should say that he responds as an artist, as a writer sensing some interesting material, a collector himself encountering an exotic new specimen:

> I stubbornly persisted in questioning her: "Can you recall when and where this strange passion of yours began?"
> I had a hard time making myself understood; finally I succeeded. But then she replied in a deeply sad tone, even, as near as I can recall, turning her eyes away from me: "I don't know . . . I don't remember." (94–95)

And he turns to drawing his conclusion, to two sentences that might have ended the piece, two sentences that reflect the same detached interest:

> What bizarre things can be found in a large city, when one knows how to walk around and look for them! Life swarms with innocent monsters. (95)

The poem could well have ended here, on the note of bemusement that concludes many of the pieces in *Paris Spleen*. And if it did end here, it would still be a remarkable piece, infused with various levels of irony and marked by a subtle implicit connection between the narrator and the perverse streetwalker, between the artist and the prostitute, between two sad "collectors."

But, crucially for the artistic and moral scheme of *Paris Spleen,* the poem does not end here, for at this point the narrator ceases to play the role of the ironic observer; indeed, the intensity of what is to come justifies one in hearing not a narrator but the poet himself. Probably because he does see that implicit connection between himself and the doomed, unhappy woman, because he does see himself implicated in her, he feels an onrush of anguish and turns to a prayer, as he did in "At One in the Morning":

> —O Lord, my God! You the Creator, you the Master; you who have made both Law and Liberty; you the sovereign who permits, you the judge who pardons; you who are filled with motives and causes, and who have perhaps put the taste for horror in my spirit in order to convert my heart, like the healing that comes from the tip of a knife blade; Lord, have pity, have pity on the madmen and madwomen! O, Creator! Can they seem to be monsters in the eyes of you who alone know why they exist, how they *were made* and how they *might have been made otherwise*? (95)

There is no detachment or irony in this emotional outpouring. Unlike the prayer of "At One in the Morning," this one is a plea not just for himself but for the others, for all the "monsters." Unlike the sentimentalizing of Victor Hugo, Baudelaire's emotion is raw and real, a mixture of pity and horror, of sympathy and even of fear. In this raw cry, the poet fully establishes his moral stance, the response that modern life demands; here is the perspective the whole collection has been working toward. What could follow such an epiphanic moment but the profoundly somber "Any Where Out of the World" (number 48), where the soul can only groan for deliverance?

Yet that groan is not quite the end of *Paris Spleen;* we have two codas. In "Let's Beat Up the Poor!" the ironist seems to regain his footing, and though this piece may initially seem rather trivial in comparison—merely a replay of "The Bad Glazier"—it carries far more resonance now; its dark comedy is deepened and broadened by the poems immediately preceding it, and indeed, all the earlier poems now take on a greater moral weight. Finally we come to "Good Dogs," with its tone of utter artistic self-confidence, with a narrator who places himself in a specific, clearly identifiable literary and social world, and who, using the vocabulary of the epic, announces himself as the singer of "the dirtied dog, the poor dog, the homeless dog . . . the unlucky dogs." Those unlucky, half-starved dogs nonetheless find a way to live, and the poem celebrates that sheer life. We recall the other animals in *Paris Spleen*—the donkey of

"A Joker," the caged rat of "The Toy of the Poor," the aging "Thoroughbred," the cats whose eyes tell time in "The Clock"—and of course their human counterparts, all the dispossessed and oppressed and rejected and monstrous ones we have encountered, the artist foremost among them, resplendent now in his prize waistcoat. "Good Dogs" has the air of an artist taking a bow at the end of a performance, and like a good bow after a dazzling performance, there is an air of pride in the work.

Had Baudelaire lived longer, this would not have been the end, for he had sketched out a list of fifty further titles for the collection; *Paris Spleen* could have continued, becoming (like Byron's *Don Juan* or Whitman's *Leaves of Grass*) an open-ended project, creating its own form and structure as it went along, capable of incorporating as much as the author wished to put into it. The fact that these fifty pieces were not written is a matter of great regret (the climactic piece was to have been titled "The Pharisee's Prayer"), yet even though the stroke Baudelaire suffered in Belgium put an end to the *Paris Spleen* project, the collection as we have it nevertheless forms a satisfying whole. Not, of course, a narrative whole in any conventional sense, as Cheryl Krueger says of the dedication to Houssaye:

> Baudelaire's references to the serpent and to the "interminable thread of a superfluous plot" represent a rejection of the boundaries normally imposed upon *prose,* not poetry, specifically the narrative prose of the novel and the short story.[27]

In *La Fanfarlo,* Baudelaire had chafed against the constraints of plot and narrative expectations, and in the dedication of *Paris Spleen* he likewise expressed the desire to be rid of the rhythmic conventions of poetry as well as those of narrative continuity. With *Paris Spleen,* he forged a new way, exploiting the possibilities of prose while maintaining an essentially poetic approach to his material.

Critics have long tended to see *Paris Spleen* as secondary to *The Flowers of Evil,* as an occasionally interesting but lesser work. But that opinion has been changing. One of the turning points was

27. Cheryl Krueger, "Surgical Imprecision and the Baudelairean *poème en prose*," *French Forum* 27, 3 (Fall 2002), 56.

Barbara Johnson's 1979 study,[28] which employed some of the then-new techniques of deconstruction and redirected attention to *Paris Spleen* as a "second revolution" in Baudelaire's development—that is, it suggested that *Paris Spleen* can be seen not as a lesser *Flowers of Evil* but as an actual advance on it. Trying to rank order one masterpiece against another is ultimately an empty exercise, however. Perhaps it is enough to point out, as I have tried to do here, that the kaleidoscopically diverse yet coherent *Paris Spleen* deserves to be read for what it is: a relentlessly, radically honest quest for a responsible ethical and artistic stance, and one of the nineteenth century's most powerful explorations of modern life.

∞

This translation is based upon the definitive text as edited by Claude Pichois, in his Oeuvres Complètes (Paris: Gallimard, 1976). I wish to thank Jeffrey Chamberlain and Brian Daniels of George Mason University, who carefully compared my English version to the original French text, and offered many excellent suggestions; the translation is much better as a result of their efforts. Any weaknesses that remain are, of course, entirely of my own doing.

---

28. Barbara Johnson, *Défigurations du langage poètique: La seconde revolution Baudelairienne* (Paris: Flammarion, 1979). Johnson also wrote a brief essay in English that condenses her arguments, titled "Disfiguring Poetic Language," in *The Prose Poem in France: Theory and Practice,* eds. Mary Ann Caws and Hermine Riffaterre (New York: Columbia University Press, 1983), 79–95.

Paris
Spleen

To Arsène Houssaye[1]

*M*y dear friend, I send you here a little work of which no one could say that it has neither head nor tail, because, on the contrary, everything in it is both head and tail, alternately and reciprocally. Please consider what fine advantages this combination offers to all of us, to you, to me, and to the reader. We can cut wherever we like—me, my reverie, you, the manuscript, and the reader, his reading; for I don't tie the impatient reader up in the endless thread of a superfluous plot. Pull out one of the vertebrae, and the two halves of this tortuous fantasy will rejoin themselves painlessly. Chop it up into numerous fragments, and you'll find that each one can live on its own. In the hopes that some of these stumps will be lively enough to please and amuse you, I dedicate the entire serpent to you.

I have a small confession to make to you. While paging through, for at least the twentieth time, Aloysius Bertrand's famous *Gaspard of the Night*[2] (doesn't a book known to you, me, and some of our friends have every right to be called "famous"?), the idea came to me to try something similar, to apply the method he used to depict ancient life, so strangely picturesque, to modern life, or rather to *a* modern and more abstract life.

Who among us has not dreamed, in his ambitious days, of the miracle of a poetic prose, musical without rhythm or rhyme, supple enough and jarring enough to be adapted to the soul's lyrical movements, to the undulations of reverie, to the twists and turns that consciousness takes?[3]

---

1. Houssaye (1814–1896) was editor of *La Presse,* in which the first twenty poems of *Paris Spleen* appeared. On Baudelaire's relationship with him, see the Introduction (xiii).

2. Bertrand's (1807–1841) collection of prose poems appeared one year after his death. While his book may have in some ways inspired Baudelaire, the two collections are very different: Bertrand's is set in his native Dijon, and its sensibility is closer to romantic medievalism than to the modernity of Baudelaire.

3. The French word *conscience* can mean either "consciousness" or "conscience," and while the former seems the better choice here, Baudelaire is also very interested, in *Paris Spleen,* in the twists and turns that the conscience takes.

My obsession with this ideal was born primarily out of frequenting vast cities, out of the intersections of their infinite connections. You yourself, my dear friend, weren't you tempted to translate the strident shouts of the glazier into a song,[4] to express in a lyrical prose all the sorrowful hints those shouts threw upward to the garrets, rising up through the street's highest fogs?

But, to tell the truth, I fear my envy has not brought me luck. Once I had begun to work, I found out that not only did I remain very distant from my mysterious and brilliant model, but that I was creating something (if it can be called "something") altogether different, an accident in which anyone else would find cause for pride, but which can only lead to deep humiliation for one who thinks the poet's greatest honor lies in having accomplished *exactly* what he had planned to do.

Affectionately yours,
C. B.

---

4. Houssaye's prose poem "The Glazier's Song" ("La chanson du vitrier") was published in 1850 and is reprinted in *Œuvres Complètes,* ed. Claude Pichois (Paris: Gallimard, 1976), 2: 1309–11 (later citations of this text will be abbreviated OC). The poem is an expression of the narrator's solidarity with the oppressed working-man, struggling to feed his wife and seven children; the glazier, explicitly compared to Jesus Christ, is given a profound dignity. Baudelaire's "The Bad Glazier," poem 9 of *Paris Spleen,* should be read as a rejection of the easy sentimentality of Houssaye's earlier poem. It is to Houssaye's credit that he printed Baudelaire's poem in *La Presse* rather than seeing it as an insult.

1

The Foreigner

*W*ho do you love the most, enigmatic man? Your father, your mother, your sister or your brother?"

"I have neither father, nor mother, nor sister, nor brother."

"Your friends?"

"There you're using a word that to this day I've never understood."

"Your country?"

"I don't know at what latitude it's situated."

"Beauty?"

"I would willingly love it, goddess and immortal."

"Gold?"

"I hate it as you hate God."

"Well, what do you love then, extraordinary stranger?"

"I love the clouds . . . the clouds passing . . . up there . . . up there . . . the marvelous clouds!"

2

The Old Woman's Despair

*T*he shriveled little old woman felt delight in seeing the pretty baby everyone fussed over, the one everyone wanted to please; this pretty creature as fragile as she, the little old woman, and—also like her—without teeth or hair.

And she went up to the child, planning to make little smiles and cheerful faces for him.

But the frightened child struggled under the caresses of the decrepit good woman, and filled the whole house with his yelps.

Then the good old woman turned back to her eternal solitude, and she wept in a corner, saying to herself:

"Ah, for us miserable old females, the era of pleasing even the innocent ones is over; and we arouse only horror in the little children we want to love!"

3

The Artist's Confiteor[1]

*O*h, how piercing are the ends of autumn days—piercing to the point of pain! For there are, among the delicious sensations, some whose indefiniteness does not exclude intensity; and nothing has a sharper blade-point than the Infinite.

So great a pleasure to let one's gaze swim in the immensity of the sky and the sea! Silence, solitude, the incomparable chastity of that azure! A small veil shimmering on the horizon, and, in its smallness and its isolation, imitating my irremediable existence, the monotonous melodies of the waves—all these things think through me, or I through them (for, in the grandeur of reverie, the "me" is quickly lost); they think, I say, but musically, pictorially, without arguments, syllogisms, deductions.

But these thoughts, whether they come from me or spring forth from things, soon become too intense. When energy combines with voluptuousness, it creates a sickness and a salutary suffering. My too-tense nerves produce only shrill and sorrowful vibrations.

And now the depth of the sky troubles me; its limpidity exasperates me. The indifference of the sea, the immutability of the scene repulses me . . . Oh, must one either suffer eternally, or eternally flee the beautiful? Nature, you pitiless enchantress, you always victorious rival, leave me alone! Stop arousing my desires and my pride! The study of the beautiful is a duel, one that ends with the artist crying out in terror before being vanquished.

---

1. The Confiteor in Catholicism is the formal prayer confessing one's sins; note that the term is used here in a poem where God is absent, and Nature is conceived as the poet's "rival."

4

A Joker

*I*t was the explosion of the new year: a chaos of mud and snow, crossed over by a thousand coaches, sparkling with playthings and candies, swarming with greedy desires and with despairs, the sanctioned delirium of a great city, designed to trouble the mind of even the strongest of solitaries.

In the midst of all this bustle and noise, a donkey trotted along quickly, harassed by a lout armed with a whip.

As the donkey was about to turn a corner, a fine gentleman, handsomely gloved, polished and oiled, necktied cruelly and imprisoned within his fine new clothes, bowed ceremoniously before the humble beast and said, whisking off his hat: "I wish you all health and happiness!" and then turned back with a fatuous air to whomever were his comrades, as if asking them to add their approval to his own satisfaction with himself.

The donkey never saw this splendid joker, and continued zealously trotting wherever his duty was calling him.

As for me, I was suddenly seized by an immeasurable rage against this splendid imbecile, who seemed to me the incarnation of the very soul of France.

The Double Room

A room like a dream, a room truly *spiritual,* whose stagnant atmosphere is lightly tinted with pink and blue.

The soul there bathes in idleness, scented by regret and desire.

—It's a thing of the dusk, something bluish, pinkish; a sensual dream during an eclipse.

The forms of the furniture are elongated, prostrated, weakened. The furniture seems to dream; it seems endowed with a sleepwalking kind of life, like the vegetable and the mineral. The fabrics speak a mute language, like flowers, like skies, like setting suns.

On the walls, no artistic abominations. Compared with the pure dream, with the unanalyzed impression, a definite and positive art is a blasphemy. Here, everything has clarity enough, as well as the delicious obscurity of harmony.

An infinitesimal scent, of the most exquisite choosing, mixed with a very light humidity, swims through this atmosphere, where the sleeping spirit is cradled in the sensations of a hothouse.

The muslin streams abundantly over the windows and in front of the bed; it pours itself out in snowy cascades. On this bed lies the Idol, the queen of dreams. But why is she here? Who brought her? What magic power installed her on this throne of reverie and voluptuousness? What does it matter: there she is! I recognize her.

Yes, these eyes that cut through the dusk with their fire; these subtle and terrible eyes, whose frightening malice I recognize. They attract, they subjugate, they devour the gaze of anyone imprudent enough to contemplate them. I have often studied them, these black stars commanding curiosity and wonder.

To what benevolent demon do I owe my being surrounded thus by mystery, silence, peace and perfumes? O beatitude! What we generally call life, even in its happiest effusions, has nothing in common with this supreme life that I now know, and that I savor minute by minute, second by second!

No! There are no more minutes, no more seconds! Time has disappeared; now it is Eternity that reigns, an eternity of delights!

But a low, terrible knock has sounded on the door and, as in hellish dreams, I feel as if I'm being struck in the stomach with a pickaxe.

And then a specter comes in. It's a bailiff, come to torture me in the name of the law; a squalid concubine come to cry "misery" and add the trivialities of her life to the sorrows of mine; or perhaps some newspaper editor's toady come to demand the rest of the manuscript.

The paradisiacal room, the idol, the queen of dreams, the "Sylphide" as the great René[1] would say—all this magic disappeared with the Specter's brutal knock.

Horror! Now I remember! I remember! Yes! This hovel, this home of eternal boredom, is in fact my own. The same stupid furnishings, dusty, battered; the chimney without fire or even embers, dirty with spittle; the sorry windows, where the rain has traced furrows in the dust; the manuscripts, erased or incomplete; the calendar, with all the dreaded deadlines marked in pencil!

And that otherworldly perfume that intoxicated my sophisticated sensibility, alas, is replaced by the fetid odor of tobacco mixed with God knows what nauseating mildews. Now, here, you breathe only the staleness of desolation.

In this world, so cramped yet so filled with disgust, only one familiar object smiles at me: the vial of laudanum, an old and terrible friend; and like all friends, alas, generous with both caresses and betrayals.

Oh, yes! Time has come back; Time reigns like a King now; and along with that hideous old man comes all his demonic entourage of Memories, Regrets, Spasms, Fears, Anxieties, Nightmares, Rages, and Neuroses.

I assure you that the seconds are now strongly, solemnly accentuated, and each one, springing forth out of the clock, says: "I am Life, intolerable, implacable Life!"

---

1. Sylphide is the name that Chateaubriand gives to the muse-like woman in *Memories from Beyond the Grave* (*Mémoires d'outre-tombe*, 1849–1850); this figure recurs in his works, including *René* (1802), where she appears but is unnamed.

There is only one single Second in human life whose mission is to announce good news, the *good news* that provokes an inexplicable fear in each of us.

Yes! Time reigns; he has reasserted his brutal tyranny. And he pushes me along as if I were an ox, with his double-edged cattle prod: "Come on, you donkey! Sweat, slave! Live on, damned one!"

6

To Each His Chimera[1]

*U*nder a wide gray sky, on a great dusty plain with neither pathways nor grass nor thistles nor nettles, I came upon a number of men who walked along bent over.

Each of them carried on his back an enormous Chimera, heavy as a sack of flour or coal, or the backpack of a Roman foot soldier.

But the monstrous beast was not an inert weight; on the contrary, it surrounded and oppressed the man with its elastic and powerful muscles; with its two great claws it clasped the chest of its mount; and its mythical head rose up over the man's head, like one of those horrific helmets that ancient warriors hoped would increase the enemy's sense of terror.

I questioned one of the men, and I asked him where they were going in this condition. He replied that he didn't know at all, neither he nor the others; but that apparently they were all headed somewhere, as they were all driven by an irresistible need to walk.

A curious thing worth noting: None of these travelers seemed to be troubled by the ferocious beast hanging around his neck and attached to his back; it was as if each considered it a part of himself. All these weary, serious faces revealed no sense of despair; under the splenetic dome of the sky, feet plunged into a dusty soil as desolate as the sky, they marched onward with the resigned look of those condemned to eternal hope.

And the whole retinue passed by me, soon sinking into the hazy horizon, into the region where the planet's rounded surface slips away from the curious human gaze.

And for a few seconds I stubbornly tried to understand this mystery; but soon an irresistible Indifference crashed down upon me, and I was more heavily burdened than they were by their crushing Chimeras.

---

1. The chimera, in classical myth, was a monster, variously depicted as part goat, part lion, part snake. But the term also suggests an illusion or obsession.

7

The Fool and Venus

*W*hat a fine day! The vast park grew faint under the burning eye of the sun, like youth under the domination of Love.

The universal ecstasy of things was not expressed by any sound; the waters themselves seemed to be asleep. Entirely unlike human celebrations, here the orgy was a silent one.

It was as if a steadily expanding light made objects sparkle more and more; as if the excited flowers burned with the desire to rival the sky's azure with the energy of their own colors, and as if the heat, making scents visible, caused them to mount up toward the stars like steam.

However, amid this universal enjoyment, I caught sight of one afflicted creature.

At the feet of a colossal Venus, one of those artificial fools, one of those voluntary buffoons assigned to amuse kings when Remorse or Ennui have overcome them, tricked out in a gaudy, ridiculous costume, wearing horns and bells on his head, pressed up against the pedestal and raised his tear-filled eyes to the immortal Goddess.

And his eyes said: "I am the least of humans and the most solitary, deprived of love and friendship, and thus inferior to the most imperfect of animals. But still I was created, I too, to perceive and feel immortal Beauty! Ah, Goddess! Have pity on my sorrow and my madness!"

But the implacable Venus with her eyes of marble only gazed out at something, I don't know what, in the distance.

The Dog and the Vial

*M*y splendid dog, my good dog, my dear little doggie, come here and sniff this superb perfume, purchased from the finest perfume maker in the city."

And the dog wagged his tail, the sign, I take it, among these poor creatures of a laugh or smile, and approached, poking his wet nose with curiosity into the opened vial—and then, suddenly recoiling in fright, he barked at me, as if in reproach.

"Ah, you miserable dog, if I had offered you a packet of excrement, you would have inhaled its odor with delight and maybe even devoured it. In this respect you, unworthy companion of my sad life, resemble the public, to whom one must never present the delicate scents that only exasperate them, but instead give them only dung, chosen with care."

The Bad Glazier

*T*here are some purely contemplative personalities, entirely unsuited to action, which nevertheless sometimes, under the spell of a mysterious, unknown impulsion, spring into action with a rapidity of which they would not have believed themselves capable.

The sort of man who, fearing that the concierge may have some distressing news for him, lurks like a coward outside his own door for an hour without daring to enter; the sort who holds on to a letter for two weeks without opening it, or who takes six months before he can bring himself to accomplish some task that has needed doing for a year—and then finds himself abruptly hurled into some precipitous act, shot like an arrow from a bow. The moralist and the doctor, who pretend to know everything, cannot explain the origin of this sudden insane energy that arises in such idle, sensual natures, and how, incapable of accomplishing the simplest and most necessary things, they find at a certain moment an abundance of courage for performing the most absurd and even dangerous acts.

One of my friends, the most inoffensive dreamer who ever lived, set fire to a forest once in order to see, he said, if fire spread as rapidly as people said it did. Ten times in a row, it didn't; but the eleventh time, it worked all too well.

Another one would light up a cigar next to a cask of gunpowder, *just to see, to know, to tempt fate,* to force himself to prove he has the energy to play the gambler, to feel the pleasures of anxiety, or for no reason, for a whim, for lack of anything better to do.

This is the kind of energy that springs out of boredom and daydreaming; and those in whom it manifests itself so unexpectedly are in general, as I've said, the most indolent and dreamiest of beings.

Another, so timid that he lowers his eyes even when other men look at him, that he has to gather all the forces of his will just to enter a café or walk past a theatre's box office, where the ticket sellers seem to him to be invested with the majesty of Minos, Aeacus, and Rhadamanthus,[1] will suddenly leap up and throw his arms around the neck of an old man passing him on the street, and will embrace him enthusiastically in front of the startled crowd.

Why? Because . . . because that particular physiognomy was irresistibly appealing to him? Perhaps; but it is more plausible to assume that he himself doesn't know why.

I have more than once been the victim of such crises and impulses, which give us grounds for believing that malicious Demons slip inside us, forcing us to carry out, unknown to ourselves, their most absurd desires.

One morning I got up sullen, depressed, bored with my laziness, and driven, I felt, to do something great, to perform some fine act; and, alas, I opened the window!

(Do observe, I beg you, that the impulse to play a prank in some people is not the result of a careful or conscious plan but of a chance inspiration, and it is closely allied, if only through the ardor of the impulse, to that humor called hysterical by the doctors and satanic by those who think a little more deeply than the doctors, which impels us, unresisting, toward any number of inappropriate actions.)

The first person I saw in the street below was a glazier whose piercing, discordant cry[2] rose up to me through the heavy, foul Parisian air. It would be entirely impossible to say why the sight of this poor man filled me with a hatred as sudden as it was despotic.

"Hey! Hey!" I called to him to come up. Meanwhile I reflected, not without some delight, that my room being on the seventh floor and the stairway being very narrow, the man would have some trouble in managing his ascent, and that he would find his fragile merchandise getting knocked around at several points along the way.

Finally he arrived: I closely examined all his panes, and I said to him: "What? You have no colored glass? No pink glass, no red, no blue, no magic panes, no panes of paradise? You impudent fool! You dare to stroll around the neighborhoods of the poor, and you don't

---

1. Three awe-inspiring judges of the classical underworld.

2. In Houssaye's poem "The Glazier's Song," the cry of the glazier forms a refrain that arouses pity in the narrator. See note 4, p. 4.

even have panes that would make life look beautiful!" And I pushed him back to the stairway, where he stumbled and grunted.

I went to my balcony and picked up a small flowerpot, and when the man reappeared out of the doorway below, I let my war machine fall straight down on the back edge of his pack; the shock knocked him over backward, and he ended up breaking, under his own back, the whole of his pathetic ambulatory fortune, with all the magnificent noise of a crystal palace shattered by lightning.

And drunk with my madness, I cried out to him furiously, "Make life beautiful! Make life beautiful!"

Crazy jokes like this are not without their peril, and often one has to pay dearly for them. But what does an eternity of damnation matter to someone who has discovered an infinity of joy within a single second?

10

At One in the Morning

*F*inally, alone! All you can hear now are the wheels of a few late, weary hackney cabs. For a few hours, we'll have silence, if not rest. Finally! The tyranny of the human face[1] has disappeared, and for now my only sufferings will be of my own making.

Finally! I am now allowed to relax in a bath of shadows! But first, a double turn of the lock: I feel as if this extra turn of the key will strengthen my solitude and fortify the barricades that now separate me from the world.

Horrible life! Horrible city! Let us review the day's events: saw several men of letters, one of whom asked me if one could get to Russia by land (he evidently took Russia for an island); argued at length with the editor of a magazine, who responded to every objection with, "Here, we stand for respectability," which implies that all the other magazines are run by rogues; greeted some twenty individuals, of whom fifteen are entirely unknown to me; shook hands in about the same proportions, and without having taken the precaution of buying gloves; to kill time during a rain shower, went up to see a cheap dancer who begged me to design her a costume for playing "Vee-nis"; paid my court to a theater director who said, in the course of dismissing me, "You'd do well to make the acquaintance of Z; he's the dullest, stupidest, and most celebrated of all my writers, so with him you might amount to something. Talk to him, and then we'll see"; prided myself (why?) on several base acts that I never performed, and denied like a coward several other misdeeds that I in fact carried out with joy—delight in boasting, crime against human decency; refused an easy favor to a friend, and wrote a recommendation for a perfect fool—oof! Are we done?

Discontent with everything, discontent with myself, I would really like to redeem myself, to feel a bit of pride in the silence and

---

1. Thomas De Quincey used this phrase in his *Confessions of an English Opium-Eater* (1822), a book Baudelaire translated as part of his own book *Artificial Paradises* (*Les paradis artificiels,* 1860).

solitude of the night. Souls of those I have loved, souls of those I have sung, strengthen me, support me, distance me from the lie and the corrupting vapors of the world, and you, my Lord God! Give me the grace to produce a few beautiful lines to prove to myself that I am not the least of men, that I am not inferior to the ones I despise!

11

The Wild Woman and the Little Mistress

*R*eally, my dear, you're wearing me down; your complaining is pitiless, out of all proportion. To hear your sighing, anyone would think you suffer more than those sixty-year-old gleaners, or those old beggar women who gather up crusts of bread outside tavern doors.

"If your sighs at least expressed remorse, they would do you some honor; but they only end in revealing that you're sated with living well, and that you're exhausted with repose. And then, you pour out a never-ending stream of babble: 'Love me well! I need that so badly! Console me this way, caress me that way!' Look, I want to try to get you back to health; and maybe we can find the way, at the cost of two sous, within a nearby fair.

"Consider carefully, please, that solid iron cage within which, howling like one of the damned, shaking the bars like an orangutan crazed by its exile, imitating to perfection now the circular pacing of a tiger and now the stupid waddle of a polar bear, rattles the hairy monster whose shape is vaguely reminiscent of your own.

"This monster is one of those animals that one generally calls 'my angel'!—that is, a woman.[1] The other monster with her, the one with a stick in his hand, shrieking at the top of his voice, is a husband. He has shackled his lawful wife like a beast, and he displays her in the suburbs on fair days—with the officials' permission, naturally.

"Pay careful attention! See the voracity (perhaps not simulated!) with which she rends living rabbits and the cheeping chickens that her keeper throws to her. 'Come now,' he says to her, 'you don't have to eat it all at once,' and with these wise words he cruelly snatches away her prey, leaving little threads of the guts still hooked to the teeth of the ferocious beast—the woman, I mean.

---

1. The "wild woman" was a common attraction at fairs in the nineteenth century; the woman would be displayed in a cage, as imagined here, eating raw meat.

"Look! A nice smack of the stick to calm her down!—for she darts her eyes, crazed with lust, on the snatched food. Good God! That stick is no stage prop; did you hear the thud of her flesh, despite the mat of false hair? And with her eyes starting practically out of her head, she now howls *more naturally.* In her rage, she seems to shimmer all over, like iron when you beat it.

"Such are the conjugal ways of these two descendants of Adam and Eve, these works of your hands, O my God! This woman is genuinely miserable, although, perhaps, the titillating pleasures of celebrity are not unknown to her. There are worse, irremediable miseries, and with no compensations. But in the world into which she has been thrown, it has never crossed her mind that a woman might deserve any other fate.

"And now, back to us, my precious one! Considering the hells that people this world, what do you expect me to think of your particular pretty hell, you who never recline against any material rougher than your own skin, and who eat only cooked meats, carved into morsels for you by a doting servant?

"And how should I take these little sighs that swell your perfumed breast, my hardy little flirt? And all these affectations picked up from books, and this untiring melancholy, designed to arouse a sentiment quite different from pity in the spectator? Really, I sometimes feel the urge to teach you what real misery is.

"To see you this way, my delicate beauty, your feet in the mud and your eyes turned ethereally to the sky, as if asking it to deliver you a King, anyone would take you for a young frog invoking the ideal. If you despise the current King (which is me right now, as you very well know), beware the next one, *who will chew you up, swallow you, and kill you at his pleasure!*[2]

"I may be a poet, but I am not as much a dupe as you would like to believe, and if you weary me too often with your *precious* whining, I will treat you like a *wild woman,* or I'll toss you out the window like an empty bottle."

---

2. Baudelaire alludes here to La Fontaine's fable, "The Frogs Who Asked for a King" (*Fables* III.4, 1668).

12

Crowds

Not everyone is capable of immersing himself in the multitude as in a bath: enjoying the crowd is an art; and the only ones who can make a feast of vitality out of the human race are those who, in their cradles, had a fairy breathe into them a taste for disguise and masks, hatred for home life, and the passion for travel.

Multitude, solitude: terms that are equivalent and interchangeable for the active and fertile poet. He who doesn't know how to people his solitude will not know how to be solitary in a busy crowd.

The poet enjoys this incomparable privilege, that he can be, just as he likes, either himself or someone else. Like those wandering souls in search of a body, he enters, whenever he likes, into the characters of everyone. For him alone, everything is unoccupied, and if certain places appear to him to be shut, it is only because in his view they aren't worth the trouble of visiting.

The solitary, pensive walker finds a singular intoxication in this universal communion. The one who weds himself to the crowd enjoys feverish pleasures denied to the egoist, who is locked up like a safe, and also denied to the lazy one, as self-confined as a mollusk. He adopts as his own all the professions, all the joys and all the miseries that circumstances present to him.

The thing that people call love is so small, so restrained, so weak compared to this ineffable orgy, to this holy prostitution of the soul that gives itself entirely, all its poetry and charity, to the unexpected as it arises, to the unknown that turns up.

It is good sometimes to teach the fortunate ones of this world, if only to humble their stupid pride for an instant, that there is a happiness superior to theirs, greater and more refined. The founders of colonies, the shepherds of peoples, the missionary priests exiled to the edge of the world, no doubt know something of these mysterious intoxications; and in the bosom of the vast family that their genius has created for them, they must laugh sometimes at those who lament their fate so troubled and their lives so chaste.

13

The Widows

*V*auvenargues[1] says that in the public parks there are pathways haunted principally by disappointed ambition, by unlucky inventions, by aborted successes, by broken hearts, by all the tumultuous and closed-down souls in whom the last sighs of a storm still rumble, and who recoil from the insolent gaze of the happy and the idle. These shady retreats are the gathering places of those crippled by life.

Above all, poets and philosophers like to direct their avid conjectures toward these places. Here there is certain sustenance. For, if there is one place they disdain to enter, as I just implied, it is above all the pleasure of affluence. That place of empty turbulence has nothing to attract them. On the contrary, they feel themselves irresistibly drawn toward everything that is weak, ruined, afflicted, orphaned.

The trained eye is never deceived. In these rigid or beaten-down features, in these hollow, dull eyes, or eyes still shining with the last light of the struggle, in these deep and numerous furrows, in these slow or broken gaits, it deciphers at once the innumerable legends of love betrayed, of devotion misconstrued, of efforts unpaid, of hunger and cold humbly, silently endured.

Have you sometimes noticed widows on lonely benches, impoverished widows? Whether they are in mourning or not, it's easy to recognize them. And besides, in the mourning of the poor there is always something missing, an absence of harmony that would render them more heartbreaking. They are forced to stint on their grief. The rich carry their grief in full view.

---

1. Luc de Clapiers, Marquis de Vauvenargues (1715–1747), an impoverished aristocrat who died of tuberculosis, wrote a series of maxims and reflections that enjoyed a new popularity in the mid-nineteenth century. A new edition of his works was published in 1857 and included a piece called "Hidden Miseries" ("Sur les misères cachées"), in which the narrator observes how unlucky and impoverished individuals seek out the great public parks, in order to escape from the view of happier people.

Which is the saddest and most affecting widow, the one who pulls along a toddler by the hand, with whom she cannot share her thoughts, or the one who is entirely alone? I don't know . . . It happened once that I followed for long hours one of the old, afflicted ones of this type; this one was rigid, straight-backed, under a worn old shawl, her whole being radiating a proud stoicism.

She was evidently condemned by an absolute solitude to the habits of an old celibate, and the masculine character of her ways added a mysterious piquancy to their austerity. I can't say in what miserable café she lunched, or how. I followed her to a public reading room; and I observed her for a long time as she searched in the newspapers, with active eyes that had once been burned by tears, for some news of an urgent, personal interest.

Finally, in the afternoon, under a charming autumn sky, one of those skies from which regrets and memories descend in multitudes, she sat off to the side in a park to listen, away from the crowd, to one of those concerts of regimental music that so please the Parisian people.

This was, no doubt, the little fling of this innocent old woman (or of this purified old woman), the well-earned consolation for one of those heavy days with no friend, no conversation, no joy, no confidante, that God allowed to weigh down on her for perhaps many years!—three hundred and sixty-five days a year.

A different one:

I cannot keep myself from casting a curious, if not entirely sympathetic, glance at the crowd of pariahs who press up against the barriers at a public concert. The orchestra pours out into the night songs of rejoicing, of triumph or of delight. Dresses trail and glitter; glances are exchanged; the idle, worn out from doing nothing, strut about, pretending to relish the music indolently. Here there is nothing but wealth, nothing but happiness; nothing that does not breathe and inspire a carefree pleasure in letting oneself live; nothing, except the sight of that mob over there leaning against the outer barrier, picking up a shred of music for free, thanks to the wind, and watching the glittering hothouse within.

It's always interesting to see the joys of the wealthy reflected in the eyes of the poor. But that day, looking out across these people wearing their working smocks and their calico, I saw one whose nobility made a striking contrast with all the surrounding vulgarity.

It was a tall, majestic woman, with so noble an air about her that I cannot recall seeing its like even in the collections of aristocratic beauties of the past. The perfume of lofty virtue emanated from her whole person. Her face, sad and thin, was in perfect accord with the formal mourning clothes she wore. And she too, like the plebeians among whom she stood and whom she did not even see, she was watching the luminous world with deep interest, and she listened while gently nodding her head.

A singular vision! "Certainly," I said to myself, "her poverty, if it is poverty, doesn't need to resort to that sordid economizing; that noble face is the proof of it. But why does she willingly remain in a milieu like that, where she stands out like a bright stain?"

But as I passed closer to her out of curiosity, I thought I saw the reason. The tall widow was holding the hand of a child, dressed in black like herself; reasonable as the price of entry was, that price might suffice to pay for one of the little one's needs or, better yet, for a luxury or a toy.

And she will walk home, lost in her own thoughts and dreams, alone, always alone; for a child is noisy, selfish, neither gentle nor patient; and he cannot, like an actual animal, like the dog or the cat, serve as a confidante for lonely sorrows.

14

The Old Mountebank

*E*verywhere the holiday crowd stretched out, spread out, had their fun. It was one of those festivals that the street performers, the acrobats, the animal trainers, the traveling peddlers, have always depended on to make up for the year's harder times.

On days like this it seems to me that the people forget everything, both the good times and the hard work; they became like children. For the little ones, it's a day off, the horror of school held at bay for twenty-four hours; for the bigger ones, it's a truce declared with life's malignant powers, a brief rest from endless contention and struggle.

Even the society man and the man engaged in spiritual labors find it difficult to escape the influence of this common jubilee. Without wanting to, they absorb their part of the carefree atmosphere. As for myself, like a true Parisian, I never fail to inspect all the booths that line the streets on these solemn occasions.

And in fact they compete with each other vigorously: they squall, bellow, howl. It was a blend of shouts, of clanging brass and exploding rockets. The red-queued acrobats and performing fools contorted their sunburnt faces, weathered by wind, rain and sun. With all the confidence of actors confident of their effects, they tossed out clever phrases and jokes, a comedy as staid and predictable as Molière's. The strongmen, proud of their enormous limbs, with foreheads and skulls resembling an orangutan's, lounged about majestically in their tights, laundered the day before for the occasion. The dancers, beautiful as fairies or princesses, tumbled and capered, their skirts sparkling under the glow of lanterns.

Everything was light, dust, shouts, joy, uproar; some spent while others gained, both equally happy. Children tugged on their mothers' skirts to obtain a stick of sugar, or climbed up on their fathers' shoulders to see more clearly some magician as dazzling as a god. And everywhere, dominating all the scents, circulated the odor of frying fat, like the festival's incense.

At the end, at the extreme end of the rows of booths, as if he had exiled himself in shame from all these splendors, I saw an old mountebank, stooped, frail, decrepit, a ruin of a man, leaning against the pole of his hovel; a hovel more impoverished than that of the most brutal savage, where two candle ends, sputtering and smoking, revealed all too well the booth's poverty.

Everywhere, joy and gain and indulgence; everywhere the assurance of tomorrow's bread; everywhere the frenetic explosion of vitality. Here, absolute misery, misery costumed, to heighten the horror, in laughable rags, where necessity more than art had introduced the contrast. He didn't laugh, the miserable one! He didn't weep, he didn't dance, he didn't gesture, he didn't shout; he sang no song, neither gay nor sorrowful; he didn't beg. He was silent and motionless. He had renounced, he had abdicated. His destiny was fixed.

But what a profound, unforgettable gaze he passed upon the crowd and the lights, whose pulsing tide ended a few steps from his repulsive poverty! I felt my throat tightened by the terrible grasp of hysteria, and I felt as if my own gaze was clouded by rebellious tears that would not fall.

What to do? What good would it do to ask the unlucky man what curiosities, what marvels he had to show me in these rank shadows, behind that shredded curtain? And in fact, I didn't dare; and, though the reason for my timidity may make you laugh, I swear that I feared humiliating him. Finally, I collected myself, and decided to place some money on one of his planks as I walked by, hoping he would understand my intention, when some unknown impetus caused a sudden surge of the crowd, and swept me far away from him.

And, taking myself back home, obsessed with this vision, I tried to analyze my sudden sadness, saying to myself: I have just seen the very image of the aging man of letters who has outlived the generation he had brilliantly amused; of the old poet without friends, without family, without children, degraded by his poverty and by public ingratitude, standing in the booth the forgetful world no longer wants to enter!

15

Cake

I was traveling. The landscape in which I found myself was of an irresistible nobility and grandeur. Something of it no doubt passed at that moment into my soul. My thoughts took flight with a lightness equal to the atmosphere's; the vulgar passions, such as hatred and profane love, appeared now as far away as the clouds floating in the depths of the abysses far below my feet; my soul felt as vast and as pure as the dome of the sky surrounding me; the memory of terrestrial things came to my heart weakened and diminished, like the sound of bells on invisible cattle grazing far, far away on the slopes of another mountain. Across the still little lake, black from its immense depths, passed sometimes the shadow of a cloud, like the reflection of a winged giant's cloak flying across the sky. And I recall that that solemn, rare sensation, caused by that great, perfectly silent movement, filled me with a joy mixed with fear. In short, I felt, thanks to the thrilling beauty around me, at perfect peace with myself and with the universe; I believe that, in my perfect beatitude and in my complete forgetting of all earthly evil, I even came to feel that those newspapers that claim man is born good were not so ridiculous.—But when the incurably material renewed its demands, I thought of soothing my fatigue and addressing the appetite caused by so long a climb. I took a large piece of bread out of my pocket, a leather cup, and a flask of a certain elixir that pharmacists sold in those days to tourists, and which could be mixed if necessary with melted snow.

I calmly began slicing my bread, when a very slight sound made me look up. Before me stood a little creature, ragged and disheveled, whose hollow eyes, savage and as if imploring, were fixed on the piece of bread. And I heard him sigh with a low, hoarse voice, the word "cake"! I couldn't help laughing at the term with which he honored my simple white bread, and I cut a generous slice and offered it to him. He approached slowly, never taking his eyes off the object of his envy; then, snapping the piece up with his hand, he retreated quickly, as if he feared my offer had not been sincere, or that I already had regretted it.

But at the same moment he was bowled over by another little savage who seemed to come out of nowhere, and so perfectly similar to the first that he could have been his twin brother. Together they rolled about in the dirt, fighting over the precious prey, neither one apparently willing to give up half to his brother. The first one, frustrated, gripped the second by the hair; the latter seized the former's ear in his teeth, and spat out a small bloody morsel with a superb curse in patois. The legitimate possessor of the cake tried to sink his fingernails into the eyes of the usurper; in turn, the latter applied all his force to strangle his adversary with one hand, while with the other he tried to slip the prize of the combat into his pocket. But revived by despair, the vanquished one gathered his strength and managed to knock the conqueror to the ground by means of a head butt to the stomach. But why describe an ugly battle that lasted in fact far longer than their childlike stature would seem to have predicted? The cake traveled from hand to hand and went from one pocket to another in an instant; but, alas, it also changed in volume; and when finally, worn out, gasping for breath, bloodied, they stopped only because they could no longer go on, there was in fact nothing left to fight over; the piece of bread had disappeared, dispersed into crumbs indistinguishable from the grains of sand with which it was now mixed.

This spectacle had muddied the landscape for me, and the calm joy my soul had enjoyed before the arrival of these little men had entirely disappeared; I remained saddened for quite a while, repeating to myself: "So there is, then, a superb country where bread is called *cake,* a delicacy so rare that it is enough to engender a literally fratricidal war!"

16

The Clock

*T*he Chinese can tell the time in the eyes of cats.[1]
    One day a missionary, strolling through a suburb of Nankin, realized that he had forgotten his watch, and he asked a little boy what time it was.

The ragamuffin of the Celestial Empire hesitated at first; then on second thought he replied, "I'll go find out for you." A few moments later he returned, carrying a very fat cat, and looking the cat, as the saying goes, in the whites of its eyes, he declared without hesitation: "It's not quite noon." Which was correct.

As for me, when I bend toward my beautiful Féline,[2] so well named, who is at once the honor of her sex, the pride of my heart, and the perfume of my spirit—whether it be night, whether it be day, in full light or in opaque shadow—in the depths of her adorable eyes I always see the hour distinctly, always the same hour, an hour vast, solemn, and grand as space, without divisions into minutes and seconds—a motionless hour unmarked by the clocks, but light as a sigh, rapid as the blink of an eye.

And if some troublemaker comes to disturb me while my gaze is fixed on this delicious clock face, if some dishonest and intolerant Genie, some Demon of bad timing comes to say to me, "What are you looking at there so attentively? What are you seeking in the eyes of this creature? Do you see the hour there, you idle, wasteful mortal?"—I would reply without hesitation: "Yes, I see the hour; it is Eternity!"

---

1. An anecdote similar to this one is in Père Huc's *The Chinese Empire* (1851), where the author explains the phenomenon with reference to the cats' pupils being dilated by sunlight.

2. Scholars are unsure who Féline was, but this was evidently a nickname for a real woman Baudelaire knew, for there is a surviving copy of *The Flowers of Evil* inscribed by him to "my very dear Féline. . . ." But contemporary readers would not have known that, and the text itself is ambiguous enough to allow Féline to be the name of a cat. In the 1857 version, the line read, "As for me, when I pick up my good cat, my dear cat. . . ."

Now, Madame, isn't this a worthy madrigal, as pompous as you yourself? Really, I've had so much pleasure in stitching together this pretentious gallantry that I will ask you for nothing in exchange.[3]

---

3. The final paragraph did not appear in the poem's 1857 version; it was added in 1862.

A Hemisphere in Her Hair

*L*et me breathe in long, long the fragrance of your hair, plunge my face entirely into it like a thirsty man into spring water, wave it in my hand like a scented handkerchief, to shake out memories into the air.

If you could know all that I see—all that I sense—all that I hear in your hair! My soul voyages on this perfume the way the souls of other men voyage on music.

Your hair contains a whole dream, full of sails and masts; it contains great seas, where monsoons carry me to enchanted climates, where the sky is bluer and more profound, where the atmosphere is perfumed by fruits, by leaves, and by human skin.

In the ocean of your hair, I can just glimpse a port swarming with melancholy songs, with vigorous men of all nations, with vessels of every shape outlining their subtle and complicated architectures against an immense sky of lazing, eternal heat.

In the caresses of your hair I recover the languors of long hours passed on a divan, in a room on a fine vessel, gently rocked by the imperceptible swellings of the port, among pots of flowers and casks of refreshing water.

In the hearth fire of your hair, I breathe in the odor of tobacco mixed with opium and sugar; in the night of your hair, I see the sheen of the infinite tropical azure; on the downy banks of your hair, I grow drunk with combined odors of tar, of musk and of coconut oil.

Let me bite your heavy black tresses slowly. When I chew on your elastic, rebellious hair, I feel I am eating memories.

Invitation to the Voyage

*T*here is a superb country, the country of Cockaigne, they say, that I dream of visiting with an old friend. A unique country, drowned in the fogs of our North, one that could be called the Orient of the Occident, the China of Europe, such free rein does it give to hot, capricious fantasy, and so patiently and stubbornly has fantasy sketched in its esoteric and delicate vegetation.

A true country of Cockaigne, where all is beautiful, rich, tranquil, fitting; where luxury delights to mix with order; where life is heavy and sweet to breathe; from which disorder, turbulence, and the unforeseen are banished; where happiness is wed to silence; where the cooking itself is poetic, rich and stimulating at the same time; where everything resembles you, my dear angel.

You know that feverish sickness that seizes us in our days of cold misery, that nostalgia for an unknown country, that anxiety born of curiosity? There is a country that resembles you, where everything is beautiful, rich, tranquil, and fitting, where fantasy has constructed and decorated an occidental China, where life is sweet to breathe, where happiness is wed to silence. That's where we must go live, that's where we must go die!

Yes, that's where we must go breathe, dream, and lengthen the hours by an infinity of sensations. A musician composed the *Invitation to the Waltz;*[1] where is the one who will compose the *Invitation to the Voyage* that one could present to the beloved woman, to the chosen sister?

Yes, it's in that atmosphere that living would be good—down there, where the slower hours contain more thoughts, where the clocks sound happiness with a deeper, more meaningful solemnity.

On gleaming panels, or on gilded, richly dark leather, discreetly live blissful, calm, deep paintings, like the souls of the artists who created them. Setting suns, that lend such rich color to the dining

---

1. Carl Maria von Weber composed his popular *Invitation to the Waltz* in 1819; it was orchestrated by Berlioz in 1831.

room or the salon, are screened by beautiful fabrics or by high, finely wrought windows divided into numerous panes by lead strips. The furniture is immense, curious, bizarre, and armed with locks and secrets like refined souls. The mirrors, the metals, the fabrics, the gold plate, and the pottery play a mute, mysterious symphony for the eyes; and from everything, from the corners, the gaps in the drawers, and the folds in the fabrics, a unique perfume escapes, a souvenir of Sumatra, a scent like the apartment's soul.

A true country of Cockaigne, I say, where all is rich, clean, and gleaming as a healthy conscience, as a magnificent array of cookware, as splendid wrought gold, as bright, multicolored jewelry! All the world's treasures flow in there, as if into the home of a laborer who has earned the thanks of the whole world. A unique country, superior to all others as Art is to Nature, where Nature is reshaped by dreams, where she is improved, embellished, recreated.

Let them search, let them keep searching, let them endlessly push back the limits of their happiness, these alchemists of horticulture! Let them offer prizes of sixty or a hundred thousand florins for the solution of their ambitious problems! As for me, I have found my *black tulip* and my *blue dahlia!*[2]

Incomparable flower, rediscovered tulip, allegorical dahlia, it is there, isn't it, in that beautiful country so calm and dreamlike, that we must go to live and to blossom? Wouldn't you be framed there by your own analogy, and wouldn't you be mirrored there—as the mystics would put it—in your own *correspondence?*[3]

Dreams, always dreams! And the more ambitious and delicate the soul, the more distant the dreams are from the possible. Every man carries within himself his dose of natural opium, endlessly hidden away and endlessly renewed, and between birth and death, how many hours can we count of actual joy, of deliberate and successful

---

2. Dumas' novel, *The Black Tulip,* was published in 1850; Pierre Dupont's song, "The Blue Dahlia," was included in a collection to which Baudelaire wrote a preface (1851). The two impossible flowers reprise the theme from "The Artist's Confiteor" of surpassing Nature.

3. The mystical idea that the world is a tissue of occult "correspondences" was a major theme in the works of Swedenborg (1688–1772); Baudelaire gave the idea its finest modern formulation in "Correspondences," the fourth poem in *The Flowers of Evil.*

acts? Will we ever live, will we ever pass into this tableau that my spirit has painted, this tableau that resembles you?

These treasures, this furniture, this luxury, this order, these perfumes, these miraculous flowers, they are you. And they are you, these great streams and these tranquil canals. These enormous vessels carried by the waters, all laden with riches, with the chant-like songs rising from the rigging, they are my thoughts as they sleep or ride on your breast. You conduct them gently toward the ocean that is Infinity, while reflecting the depths of the sky in the clarity of your beautiful soul—and when they grow fatigued by the swell, and are gorged with the fruits of the Orient, and return to their native port, they will be still my thoughts, enriched, and returning from the Infinite toward you.

19

The Toy of the Poor[1]

I want to suggest an innocent diversion. So few amusements involve no guilt!

When you go out in the morning, determined only to wander up and down the highways, fill your pockets with little gadgets that cost no more than a sou—like the flat puppet worked by a single string, the blacksmith beating on an anvil, the rider and his horse, with a tail that works as a whistle—and in front of taverns, or under the trees, give them out as gifts to the unknown poor children you encounter. At first, they won't dare to take them; they won't believe their good fortune. But then their hands will eagerly snatch up the present, and off they will flee, as cats do when they go far away to eat the morsel you have given them, having learned to distrust people.

Down one road, behind the gate of an enormous garden, at the back of which could be seen the whiteness of a pretty chateau struck by the sun, stood a fine and fresh child, dressed in those country clothes that are so coyly attractive.

Luxury, the absence of worry, and the habitual spectacle of wealth make these children so pretty that one would think them made from a different mold than the children of mediocrity or poverty.

Next to him on the grass lay a splendid toy, as fresh as its master, gleaming and gilded, wearing a purple outfit, covered with little feathers and glass beads. But the child was not playing with his favorite toy; instead, this is what he was watching:

On the other side of the gate, on the road, among the thistles and nettles, there was another child, dirty, puny, soot-covered, one of those pariah-animals in which an impartial eye would detect beauty if, like the eye of the connoisseur detecting an ideal painting beneath a layer of varnish, he could wash off the repulsive patina of poverty.

---

1. This poem is a revised version of an anecdote included in Baudelaire's 1853 essay, "The Morality of the Toy" ("Morale du joujou"), OC 1: 581–87.

Through this symbolic barrier separating two worlds, that of the highway and that of the chateau, the poor child was showing his own toy to the rich one, who examined it eagerly as if it were some rare and unknown object. Now, this toy that the dirty little child was provoking, tossing and shaking in a box with a grate—was a live rat! The parents, through economy no doubt, had taken the toy directly from life itself.

And the two children laughed with each other fraternally, smiling with teeth of an *equal* whiteness.

20

The Fairies' Gifts

*I*t was a great assembly of Fairies, to arrange for the distribution of gifts among all the newborns who had come into life in the past twenty-four hours.

All these ancient and capricious sisters of Destiny, all these bizarre Mothers of joy and of sorrow, were highly diverse: some seemed somber and ill-tempered; others, frisky and mischievous; some, young, who had always been young; others, old, who had always been old.

All the fathers who believed in the Fairies had arrived, each carrying his newborn in his arms.

The Gifts, the Abilities, the good Fortunes, the invincible Circumstances were heaped up beside the tribunal, like prizes on a platform at a graduation ceremony. But what was different here was that the Gifts were not recompense for effort; quite to the contrary, they were a grace accorded to someone who had not yet lived, a grace that could determine his fate and become the source of either his misery or, just as easily, his happiness.

The poor Fairies had a busy time of it, for the crowd of petitioners was very great, and the intermediary world, situated between mankind and God, must submit like ours to the terrible law of Time and all his endless offspring, the Days, the Hours, the Minutes, the Seconds.

In truth, they were as flustered as ministers on a session day, or as the pawnbrokers of the Mont-de-Piété when a national festival day mandates free redemptions. I suspect that from time to time they watched the hands of the clock just as human judges do who, on the bench since early morning, can't help but daydream about their dinner, their families, and their beloved slippers. So, if there is a little haste and randomness in supernatural justice, we should not be surprised to see that the same is sometimes true in human justice too. If we were surprised, we would be unjust judges ourselves.

Thus, some blunders were committed that day that one might consider bizarre if prudence, rather than caprice, were the distinctive, eternal characteristic of the Fairies.

And so the power of attracting wealth like a magnet was awarded to the sole heir of a very rich family who, having been endowed neither with any sense of charity nor with any longing for life's more conspicuous goods, were doomed to find themselves later on prodigiously embarrassed by their millions.

And so the love of the Beautiful and of poetic Power were given to the son of a humorless old scoundrel, a quarryman, who could not in any way help him with his skills nor alleviate the troubles of his deplorable offspring.

I forgot to mention that the process of distribution on these solemn days is not open to appeal, and that no gifts may be refused.

All the Fairies stood up, thinking their drudgery was over; for no gifts were left, no crumbs of largesse left to toss out to the flock of humans, when one brave man—a poor little tradesman, I believe— stood up and, grabbing hold of the multicolored vaporous dress of the Fairy closest to him, cried out:

"Oh, Madame! You're forgetting us! There is still my child! I don't want to have come all this way for nothing!"

The Fairy might very well have been embarrassed, because there was *nothing* left. But just then she remembered a law that was well known though infrequently applied in the supernatural world inhabited by those intangible deities, friends to humankind and often forced to adapt themselves to human passions, such as the Fairies, the Gnomes, the Salamanders, the Sylphides, the Sylphs, the Nixies, the Undins and the Undines—I mean the law that gives the Fairies in a case like this, a case where the gifts are exhausted, the ability to give one more, supplementary and exceptional, provided that she has enough imagination to create it on the spot.

Therefore, the good Fairy replied, with a self-possession befitting her rank: "I give to your son . . . I give him . . . the *Gift of pleasing!*"

"But pleasing how? Pleasing . . . ? Pleasing why?" stubbornly asked the little shopkeeper, who was evidently one of those all too common thinkers, incapable of elevating his mind to the logic of the Absurd.

"Because! Because!" replied the incensed Fairy, turning her back on him; and rejoining the procession of her peers, she said to them: "What do you think of this conceited little Frenchman, who wants to understand everything, and who, upon having obtained for his son the very best of fates, still dares to question what can't be questioned, and to debate what can't be debated?"

21

The Temptations: Or, Eros, Plutus, and Fame

*T*wo superb Satans and a She-Devil, no less extraordinary, last night ascended the mysterious stairway by which Hell mounts its assault on the weakness of the sleeping man and communicates secretly with him. And they came and posed themselves gloriously before me, standing erect like actors on a stage. A sulfurous splendor emanated from these three personages, as they loomed forward and separated themselves from the opaque depths of the night. They seemed so proud and so entirely dominant that at first I took the three of them for real gods.

The sex of the first Satan's face was ambiguous, and the soft lines and shape of his body were reminiscent of an ancient Bacchus. His beautiful, languid eyes, with their shadowy, undecided color, resembled violets still drooping with the tears of a storm, and his half-opened lips resembled a warm censer, exhaling the fine scents of a perfume shop; and every time he sighed, musky insects seemed to glow and flutter in his fiery breath.

A gleaming serpent wound around his purple tunic like a belt, and with raised head turned its glowing eyes languorously toward him. From this living belt hung, interspersed with vials of sinister liquids, shining knives and surgical instruments. In his right hand he held another vial with luminous red contents, labeled with these bizarre words: "Drink, this is my blood, the perfect cordial"; in his left was a violin that evidently aided him in singing of his pleasure and his sorrows, and in spreading the contagion of his madness during Sabbath nights.

From his delicate ankles trailed some links of a broken golden chain, and when the resulting discomfort forced him to lower his eyes toward the ground, he admired with vanity his toenails, bright and shining like well-polished gems.

He gazed upon me with inconsolably doleful eyes, brimming with an insidious intoxication, and he said to me in a musical voice: "If you wish, if you wish, I will make you the lord of souls, and you will be the master of living matter, even more than the sculptor can be of his clay; and you will know the pleasure, endlessly renewed, of escaping out of yourself and forgetting yourself in others, and of drawing in other souls, to the point where you cannot distinguish them from your own."

And I replied, "Many thanks! But I want nothing to do with that trash of other beings who, probably, are of no more value than my own poor me. And while I have plenty of shame to remember, I don't want to forget anything; and even if I didn't already know you, old monster, your mysterious cutlery, your dubious vials, the chains that bind your feet are all symbols that would explain clearly enough the drawbacks of being your friend. Keep your gifts."

The second Satan did not have that same air of smiling tragedy, nor those fine, insinuating manners, nor that delicate and perfumed beauty. This was an enormous man with a huge, eyeless face, with a heavy pot belly that sagged down to his thighs, and all his skin was gilded and illustrated, as if by tattoos, with a crowd of little, moving figures representing the numerous forms of universal misery. There were small, lanky men who were voluntarily hung from nails; there were little, skinny, malformed gnomes whose supplicating eyes begged for alms more effectively than their trembling hands; and then there were old mothers carrying sickly infants at their worn-out breasts. And there were many more.

The fat Satan rapped his fist on his immense belly, which made a long, clanking, metallic sound, ending in a vague moaning made up of numerous human voices. And he laughed, obscenely revealing his broken teeth, an enormous imbecilic laugh, as some people in every land do when they have overeaten.

And he said to me: "I can give you what will get you everything, what is worth everything, what can replace everything!" And he rapped on his monstrous stomach, as the sonorous echo made a commentary on his coarse words.

I turned away in disgust, and I replied: "I don't need, for my pleasure, the misery of anyone else; and I don't want any wealth stained, like wallpaper, with all the evils depicted on your skin."

As for the She-Devil, I'd be lying if I didn't admit that at first I found a bizarre charm in her. The only way I can define this charm is by comparing it to that of very beautiful women who are on the decline, but who grow no older, whose beauty retains the piquant magic of ruins. She was at once both imperious and awkward, and her eyes, though tired looking, still retained a fascinating force. What struck me the most was the mystery of her voice, in which I discerned the echo of the most delicious *contralti,*[1] as well as something of the huskiness of throats too long bathed in brandy.

"Do you want to know my power?" said the false goddess with her charming, paradoxical voice. "Listen."

And she put a gigantic trumpet to her lips from which hung streamers, like a toy flute, on which were the titles of all the newspapers in the universe, and through this trumpet she cried out my name, which then rolled out across space with the power of a hundred thousand thunderclaps, and resounded back to me like an echo from the most distant planet.

"Devil!" I said, half vanquished, "now that is something precious!" But as I examined the seductive harpy more attentively, I had a vague feeling that I recognized her, that I had seen her drinking somewhere with some fools I knew; and the harsh sounds of her brass had brought to my ears some vague memory of a prostituted trumpet.

So I said, with utter disdain, "Get out of here! I was not born to wed the mistress of certain men I don't wish to name."

Certainly I had the right to feel proud of my courageous self-denial. But unfortunately, I woke up, and all my strength abandoned me. "Truly," I said to myself, "I must have been deeply asleep to have displayed such scruples. Ah, if only they could come back while I was awake, I wouldn't be quite so delicate!"

And I called on them at the top of my voice, begging them to forgive me, offering to dishonor myself as often as necessary to merit their favor; but I had apparently offended them extremely, for they have never returned.

---

1. The contralto is the lowest female vocal part, midway between soprano and tenor. The She-Devil's voice is low and husky, yet musical.

22

Evening Twilight

*T*he day fades. A great calm arises within the poor spirits wearied by the day's labor; and their thoughts now take on the tender, uncertain colors of twilight.

But from the top of the mountain, a great howling reaches my balcony, coming through the high, thin clouds of the night, composed of a mass of discordant cries combined by the distance into a dismal harmony, like that of the rising tide or an awakening tempest.

Who are the unfortunate ones who are not calmed by the evening and who take, as owls do, the coming of night as a signal for their unholy witch's Sabbath? This sinister ululation comes to us from the black asylum perched on the mountain; and in the evening—as I smoke and contemplate the immense valley in repose, bristling with the houses whose every window proclaims, "Peace is here now; here is the joy of family!"—I can, when the wind blows from up there, cradle my startled thoughts on this imitation of Hell's harmonies.

Twilight excites madmen.—I remember that I had two friends who were made quite ill by twilight. The one would, at that hour, misconstrue every gesture of friendship and politeness and would savagely mistreat the first comer. I saw him throw an excellent roast chicken at a head waiter, believing he had discovered in it who knows what insulting hieroglyphic message. The evening, precursor to the deepest delights, spoiled even the most succulent things for him.

The other, having been wounded in his ambition, became progressively more bitter, more somber, more difficult as the sun set. Indulgent and friendly during the day, he was ruthless in the evening; and it was not only on others but also on himself that he would furiously unleash his twilight madness.

The first one died mad, unable to recognize his wife and his child; the second carries within himself the anxiety of a perpetual sickness, and I believe that even if he were gratified by all the honors that republics and princes can bestow, the twilight would still ignite within him that burning lust for imaginary distinctions. The night, which implants darkness within their spirits, brings light to mine; and though it is not rare for the same cause to engender two different effects, still it leaves me both intrigued and alarmed.

O night, O refreshing shadows! For me, you are the signal for an interior holy day, you are deliverance from anguish! In the solitude of the plains, in the stony labyrinths of capital cities, you, the sparkling of stars and bursting forth of street lanterns, are the fireworks of the goddess Liberty!

Twilight, how sweet and tender you are! The pink glow still trailing across the horizon, like the death struggle of a day under the conquering oppression of its night, the candelabra flames casting thick red stains on the last glories of the setting sun, the thick draperies that an unseen hand draws across the depths of the East—these are the imitations of all the complex feelings at war within the heart of the man in the solemn hours of his life.

Or, again, like one of those strange dresses dancers wear, where a somber, transparent gauze lets one glimpse beneath it the faded splendors of a once-striking skirt, in the same way as the delicious past pierces through the black present; and the wavering, scattered stars of gold and silver represent those flames of fantasy that only flare up vividly under the profound mourning of the Night.

23

Solitude

A generous-hearted journalist told me that solitude is bad for man; and in support of his thesis he cited, as nonbelievers always do, the sayings of the Church Fathers.

I know that the Devil often prefers the wilderness, and that the Spirit of murder and lust can be wondrously kindled in solitary places. But it could be possible that this solitude is only dangerous for the slothful, desultory soul who peoples it with his own passions and chimeras.

It is certain that a loudmouth, whose supreme pleasure consists in pontificating from a pulpit or a bench, would be in grave danger of going stark raving mad on Robinson's island. I don't ask of my journalist the courageous virtue of Crusoe, but I do ask him not to hurl his accusations at those who love solitude and mystery.

There are, among our chattering race, some individuals who would accept even the death penalty with little reluctance, if they were permitted to make a copious harangue from the height of the gallows without fearing that Santerre's drums would cut off their words too soon.[1]

I don't complain about them, because I see that their oratorical effusions procure pleasures for them the equal of those that others find in silence and contemplation; but I despise them.

Above all, I wish that my accursed journalist would let me amuse myself in my own way. "You don't feel, then," he asks me, with a fully evangelical nasality, "the need to share your joys?" Look at this subtle envy! He knows that I sneer at his pleasures, so he tries to insinuate himself into mine, the miserable killjoy!

---

1. In 1793, Antoine Joseph Santerre was warden for the imprisoned Louis XVI. At the execution, Santerre is said to have ordered his drummers to drown out the king's last words.

"This great evil of not being able to be alone . . ." La Bruyère says somewhere,[2] as if to shame all those who have to hurry off to a crowd in order to forget themselves, fearing they would be unable to tolerate themselves alone.

"Almost all our evils arise from being unable to stay in our rooms," said another sage, Pascal, I believe,[3] recalling thus from within his contemplative's cell all those madmen who seek out their happiness in activity and in a species of prostitution that I could term *fraternarian,* if I wanted to speak the beautiful language of my century.

---

2. Jean de la Bruyère (1645–1696) wrote a series of aphorisms collected in his *Characters* (*Les caractères,* 1688), including the one Baudelaire slightly misquotes: "All our evils come from our inability to be alone. . . ."

3. In the *Pensées,* Pascal (1623–1662) wrote, "All human misery comes from a single cause, which is our inability to remain quietly within our rooms."

24

Plans

*H*e said to himself, strolling through a great park alone: "How beautiful she would be in one of those complicated, elaborate Court gowns, in the air of a fine evening, descending the marble steps of a palace, facing onto great lawns and ponds! For she has the natural air of a princess."

Walking later down a street, he stopped in front of a print shop, and finding in a box a depiction of a tropical landscape, he said to himself: "No! A palace isn't the place where I'd like to possess her sweet life. We wouldn't be *at home* there! And those walls speckled with gold wouldn't leave any space to hang her picture; those solemn galleries don't provide any quiet corners for intimacy. Definitely, *this* place is where I have to go to cultivate my dream and my life."

And, while critically examining every detail of the print, he continued to himself: "By the seashore, a fine wood cabin, surrounded by all those bizarre, gleaming trees whose names I've forgotten . . . in the air, that intoxicating, indefinable scent . . . within the cabin, a powerful perfume of rose, of musk . . . farther off, behind our little domain, the tops of masts rocking on the ocean swells . . . around us, beyond the room lit by a pink light filtered by the blinds, decorated with cool braided mats and sensual flowers, with rare Portuguese rococo chairs made of heavy, dark wood (where she would repose so calmly, so well fanned, smoking tobacco lightly laced with opium), and beyond, on the veranda, the din of the birds drunk with light, and the chattering of little Negresses . . . and at night, for accompaniment to my dreams, the plaintive song of musical trees, the melancholy filao trees:[1] Yes, truly, *there* is the décor I've been seeking. Why did I bother with palaces?"

---

1. The filao tree, also known as the casuarina, is a tall conifer native to the tropics. Baudelaire would have encountered it on his 1841 voyage, very probably on the beaches of Mauritius—which is the setting of the following poem, "Beautiful Dorothy."

And later, as he walked down a wide avenue, he noticed a neat little inn where, from a window brightened by calico curtains, leaned out two laughing faces. And suddenly: "My mind," he said to himself, "must be a real vagabond to go seeking so far off for what is quite near. Here are pleasures and happiness in the first inn I came across, in the inn of chance, teeming with delights. A big fire, some gaudy plates, a passable supper, a hearty wine, and a big bed with blankets a bit rough but clean: what's better than this?"

And returning home alone, at the hour when the counsels of Wisdom are not drowned out by the buzzing of exterior life, he said to himself: "I have had today, in fantasy, three homes, in all of which I found equal pleasure. Why force my body to change its place, when my soul voyages with such agility? And why bother to carry out my plans, since the plan is in itself a sufficient joy?"

25

Beautiful Dorothy[1]

*T*he sun overwhelms the town with its terrible, vertical light; the sand is dazzling and the sea shimmers. The stupefied world gives up weakly and begins its siesta, a siesta like a kind of delicious death in which the sleeper, half awake, tastes the delights of his own annihilation.

But Dorothy, strong and proud like the sun, walks down the deserted street, the only living creature at that hour beneath the immense expanse of azure, casting a sharp black shadow against the light.

She moves forward softly, her thin torso swaying above her broad hips. Her light pink silk dress clings to her, a sharp contrast to her dark skin, molding perfectly to her long torso, her hollow back, her pointed breasts.[2]

Her red parasol, filtering the sunlight, projects a blood-red rouge upon her dark face.

The weight of her massive hair, almost blue, pulls her delicate head back, giving her a triumphant and indolent air. Heavy earrings warble secretly at her ears.

From time to time the ocean breeze lifts a corner of her floating skirt, revealing her gleaming, superb legs; and her feet, so like the feet of the marble goddesses that Europe shuts up in museums, faithfully imprint their form on the fine sand. For Dorothy is such a prodigious flirt that the pleasure of being admired prevails over the pride of having been emancipated, and even though she is free, she walks without shoes.

---

1. This poem is one of the few with a non-French setting; like the previous poem, it involves memories of the trip Baudelaire made to Mauritius and other islands when he was twenty years old.

2. When this poem was originally printed in the *Revue Nationale* in 1863, the editor changed this line to read ". . . molding perfectly to the shape of her body." Baudelaire responded angrily that if the editor disapproved of anything, even a comma, he should reject the entire poem, but he should not change anything, not so much as a comma.

So she moves along, harmoniously, happy to be alive, and smiling a bright smile, as if she can see a mirror far off reflecting her movement and her beauty.

At this hour, when even the dogs howl sorrowfully under the biting sun, what powerful motive could be driving the indolent Dorothy like this, beautiful and cool as bronze?

Why has she left her little cabin, so daintily decorated, where flowers and mats make a perfect boudoir at so little expense; where she takes such pleasure in combing her hair, in smoking, in being fanned or in gazing into the great feather fan mirror, while the sea, pounding the beach a hundred steps away, makes a strong, rhythmic accompaniment to her vague fantasies, and while the iron pot, where a stew of crabs, rice, and saffron is cooking, wafts its stimulating scents from the back of the courtyard?

Perhaps she plans a meeting with some young officer who, on distant shores, has heard his comrades speak of the celebrated Dorothy. Inevitably, she will implore him, simple creature, to describe the Opera Ball, and she will ask if one can go there barefooted, as at the Sunday dances where even the old Kaffir women become drunk and delirious with joy; and then, whether the beauties of Paris are all more beautiful than she is.

Dorothy is admired and cherished by all, and she would be entirely happy if she were not obliged to hoard every piaster she can to buy back her little sister who is just eleven, and who is already ripe, and so beautiful! She will undoubtedly succeed, the good Dorothy; the child's master is so greedy, too greedy to understand any beauty other than that of coins!

26

The Eyes of the Poor

*A*h, you want to know why it is that I hate you today. It will be, no doubt, harder for you to understand it than for me to explain it; for you are, I believe the finest example of feminine impermeability on the face of the earth.

We had passed a long day together, one that seemed short to me. We had promised that we would share all our thoughts that day, and that our two souls henceforth would be one—a dream with nothing original in it, after all, except that although everyone has dreamed it, no one has ever realized it.

That evening, a little weary, you wanted to sit down in front of a new café that formed the corner of a new boulevard, still piled with rubble but already gloriously displaying its unfinished splendors. The café was glittering. The gaslight itself seemed to feel all the excitement of a premiere, and with all its might it lit up walls blindingly white, the dazzling arrays of mirrors, the gold cornices and decorative moldings, with the plump-faced page boys pulled along by dogs on leashes, the laughing women with falcons perched on their wrists, the nymphs and goddesses carrying fruits on their heads, pâtés and game birds, the Hebes and the Ganymedes[1] holding out their arms to offer little jars of mousse or a multicolored obelisk of ice cream; all of history and all of mythology reduced to pimping for gluttony.

Directly in front of us on the edge of the street, as if planted there, stood a good fellow of about forty years, with a wearied face and graying beard, holding a little boy by one hand and carrying a smaller one, not yet strong enough to walk, on his other arm. He was playing the nanny role, and had taken his children out for an evening walk. All of them in rags. The three faces were

---

1. Hebe and Ganymede were female and male, respectively, cupbearers to Zeus. Hebe was Zeus' daughter, while Ganymede was a human boy so beautiful that Zeus carried him off to Olympus with him.

extraordinarily serious, and all six eyes fixedly contemplated the new café with an equal wonder, but nuanced according to age.

The father's eyes said: "How fine it is! How fine it is! It's as if all the gold in the poor world has come here to decorate these walls." The little boy's eyes: "How fine it is! How fine it is! But this is a place that won't admit people like us." As for the smallest one's eyes, they were too fascinated to express anything beyond a stupefied and profound joy.

The songwriters say that pleasure refines the soul and softens the heart. The songs were right that evening, in my case. I was not only moved by this family of eyes, but I felt a little ashamed of our glasses and carafes, so much bigger than our thirsts. I turned my gaze to your eyes, my love, in order to read *my* thoughts there; I plunged deeply into your eyes, so beautiful and so bizarrely soft, into your green eyes, those eyes inhabited by Caprice and inspired by the Moon, and then you said to me: "Those people over there are intolerable, with their eyes open wide as gates! Couldn't you ask the head waiter to get them out of here?"

So difficult it is to understand each other, my dear angel, and so incommunicable are our thoughts, even between people who love each other!

27

A Heroic Death

*F*ancioulle was an admirable jester, practically one of the Prince's friends. But for those people whose career condemns them to the comic, serious things have a fatal attraction, and while it may appear bizarre that ideas of patriotism and liberty should take despotic possession of a comic actor's brain, Fancioulle one day entered into a conspiracy conjured up by some malcontented noblemen.

There exist everywhere decent men who will denounce to the reigning power those melancholic sorts of individuals who wish to depose princes and bring about a change of scene for a society, without bothering to consult it. The lords in question were arrested, as was Fancioulle, and condemned to a certain death.

I can easily believe that the Prince was somewhat upset to find his favorite actor among the rebels. The Prince was neither better nor worse than any other one; but an excessive sensibility led him, in many cases, to be more cruel and more despotic than his peers. A passionate lover of the fine arts, and an excellent connoisseur besides, he was truly insatiable when it came to his pleasures. Indifferent enough when it came to men and morality, and a true artist himself, the only really dangerous enemy he knew was Boredom, and the bizarre efforts he undertook either to flee or to vanquish that tyrant of the world would have certainly received, from a severe historian, the epithet of "monster," if it had been permitted in his domains to write anything that did not tend strictly toward pleasure or to shock, which is one of pleasure's most delicate forms. This Prince's greatest misfortune was that there was never a theater vast enough for his genius. There are some young Neros who suffocate under too restrictive conditions, and whose names and good intentions must remain unknown to future centuries. A careless Providence had given greater abilities than estates to this Prince.

Suddenly a rumor ran around that the sovereign wanted to show mercy to the conspirators; and the origin of this rumor was the announcement of a great pantomime, in which Fancioulle would play one of his finest, best-known roles, and in which the condemned noblemen, it was said, would also take part; a perfectly clear sign, said some of those with superficial minds, of the offended Prince's generous nature.

For a man both naturally and willfully eccentric, anything was possible, even virtue, even clemency, and especially if he hoped to discover some unknown pleasures in it. But for those who had been able, as I had, to penetrate more deeply into the depths of that strange, sick soul, it was infinitely more probable that the Prince was curious to see the quality of dramatic talents in a man condemned to death. He wanted to use the occasion to make a physiological experiment of positively *capital* interest, and to verify the extent to which an artist's habitual abilities could be altered or modified by the extraordinary situation in which he found himself; beyond that, was there any more or less fixed intention of clemency in his soul? That is a point that has never been settled.

Finally the great day came, and the little court deployed all its pomp, and it is difficult to conceive, if you haven't seen it, how much splendor the privileged class of a small state, with limited resources, can put forth for a solemn occasion. And this one was doubly solemn, first because of the wondrous luxury displayed, and secondly for the moral and mysterious interest attached to it.

Now, Fancioulle excelled especially in mute roles or ones with few words, roles that are often important in those magical dramas whose object is representing symbolically the mystery of life. He made his entrance lightly and with perfect composure, which contributed to the public belief in the likelihood of mercy and pardon.

When one says of an actor, "This is a good actor," one is using a formula that implies that beneath the character one can divine the actor—his art, his effort, his will. Now, if an actor could come to be, with regard to the character he is to portray, what the finest statues of Antiquity would be if they were miraculously animated, alive, walking, seeing, with regard to the general and confused idea of beauty—this would undoubtedly be a singular and wholly new thing. Fancioulle was on that night a perfect representation of an ideal, one that no one could doubt was living, possible, real. The jester came and went, laughed and cried and convulsed himself, all with an indestructible halo around his head, a halo invisible to everyone but visible to me, a halo that mixed together in a strange amalgam the rays of Art and the glory of a Martyr. Fancioulle introduced, by who knows what special grace, the divine and the supernatural even into the most extravagant buffooneries. My pen trembles, and the tears of an indelible emotion rise to my eyes as I try to describe that unforgettable evening to you. Fancioulle proved to me peremptorily, irrefutably, that the intoxication of Art is more adept than any other at veiling the terrors of the abyss; that genius can play at comedy on the brink of the tomb with a joy that hides the view of the tomb, lost as it is in a paradise that excludes all ideas of the tomb and of destruction.

Everyone in the audience, blasé and frivolous as they were, soon submitted to the all-powerful domination of the artist. No one thought any longer of death, or mourning, or of the supreme penalty. Each gave himself entirely to the array of delights that a living artistic masterpiece can give. Many times the vaults of the building were shaken by explosions of joy and admiration, with all the energy of rolling thunder. The Prince himself, intoxicated, joined his applause to that of his court.

However, the penetrating eye could see that his intoxication was not unmixed with something else. Did he feel outdone in his despotic power? Humiliated in his art of striking terror into people's hearts and chilling numbness into their spirits? Frustrated in his hopes and baffled in his plans? Such considerations—not exactly justified, but not absolutely unjustified—crossed my mind as I contemplated the Prince's face, on which a new pallor was ceaselessly adding itself to his customary pallor, as snow adds itself to snow. His lips clenched more and more, and his eyes were lit with an inner fire similar to that of jealousy and bitterness, even while he ostensibly applauded the talents of his old friend the strange jester, who jested at death so well. At a certain moment, I saw His Highness bend down toward a small page boy stationed near him, and whisper in his ear. The mischievous face of the handsome boy lit up with a smile; and then he abruptly left the princely box as if to carry out an urgent mission.

A few minutes later, a sharp, prolonged hissing interrupted Fancioulle in one of his best moments, tearing at both hearts and ears at once. And from the box where this unexpected disapproval had issued, a child ran hurriedly out into the corridor with muffled laughter.

Fancioulle, shaken, awoke from his dream, and first closed his eyes, then quickly opened them unnaturally wide, opened his mouth as if struggling for breath, staggered forward a bit, then backward, and then fell dead on the stage.

That hissing, striking as rapidly as a sword, had it really frustrated the executioner? Had the Prince himself foreseen the homicidal efficacy of his trick? It is permissible to doubt it. Did he miss his dear and inimitable Fancioulle? It is sweet and legitimate to believe it.

The guilty noblemen had enjoyed the comic spectacle for the last time. In that same night, they were erased from life.

Since that time, many mime actors, justly appreciated in other lands, have come to perform before the court of ***; but not one of them has ever compared with the marvelous talents of Fancioulle, nor have any of them ever risen to the same *favor.*

28

Counterfeit Money

*A*s we left the tobacco shop, my friend very carefully sepa-
rated and organized his change: into the left pocket of his
vest he slipped the small gold pieces; in the right, small silver ones;
in the left pocket of his pants, a handful of larger brass ones; and
finally, in the right, a silver two-franc piece that he had examined
with great attention.

"Exceptionally minute subdividing!" I said to myself.

We came across a poor beggar who held out his cap tremblingly.
I know of nothing more disconcerting than the mute eloquence of
those supplicating eyes that, for the sensitive man who knows how
to read them, contain at once so much humility and so much
reproach. There is something in them like that deeply complicated
sentiment that can be seen in the tearful eyes of dogs being whipped.

My friend's offering was considerably larger than my own, and I
said to him, "You're right to do that; after the pleasure of being sur-
prised, the next greatest is that of giving someone else a surprise." "It
was the counterfeit coin," he replied calmly, as if to justify his prodi-
gality.

But into my miserable brain, which is always busy trying to see
things as other than they appear (such is the wearisome talent with
which nature gifted me), the idea suddenly sprang up that such an
action on my friend's part was only excusable by the desire to create
a kind of event in the poor devil's life, and perhaps to see what
diverse consequences, disastrous or otherwise, a counterfeit coin
could engender when placed in the hand of a beggar. Might it not
multiply itself in real coins? Might it not, also, send him to prison?
A tavern-keeper, a butcher, for example, might have him arrested for
counterfeiting or for passing false coins. And the false coin might
just as easily become, for a small, poor speculator, the seed for sev-
eral days' riches. And so my thoughts wandered off down their own
paths, giving wings to what my friend might have been thinking,
drawing all possible deductions from all possible hypotheses.

But he abruptly deflated my reverie by repeating my own words: "Yes, you're right; there's no sweeter pleasure than surprising a man by giving him more than he hopes for."

I looked him straight in the eyes, and I was appalled to see those eyes bright with unquestionable candor. I now saw clearly that what he had intended was to do a piece of charity and at the same time to make a sort of bargain; to win both forty sous and the heart of God; to get himself into paradise thriftily; and, finally, to acquire, *gratis,* the status of a charitable man. I could almost have pardoned that criminal pleasure that I had just now assumed him capable of; I would have found it curious, peculiar, that he amused himself by compromising poor people; but I could never pardon the ineptitude of his calculations. It is never excusable to be wicked, but there is some merit in knowing that one is; and the most unredeemable vice is to do evil through stupidity.

29

The Generous Gambler

Yesterday on a crowded boulevard I felt myself brushed by a mysterious Being whom I had always wanted to meet, and whom I recognized at once, even though I had never actually seen him. He evidently felt an analogous desire with regard to me, for as he passed he gave me a meaningful wink, which I hastened to obey. I followed him closely, and soon I descended behind him into an underground dwelling, a dazzling place, glittering with a luxury unrivaled by any of the superior homes in Paris. It seemed strange to me that I could have passed this prestigious den so often without seeing its entrance. An exquisite, even heady atmosphere reigned there, which made you forget almost instantly all life's tedious horrors; there, you breathed in a somber beatitude, similar to that the lotus-eaters must have felt when, disembarking on the enchanted isle lit by the sun of an eternal afternoon, they felt arising within them, in the soothing sounds of melodious waterfalls, the desire never to see again their household gods, their wives, their children, and never again to climb the high waves of the sea.[1]

There were strange faces of men and women there, marked by a fatal beauty, which I felt I had seen before in times and countries that were now impossible to recall precisely, and which inspired more of a fraternal sympathy in me than that fear that the unknown stranger usually involves. If I wanted to try defining the peculiar expression in their gaze, I would say that I've never seen eyes that burned so energetically with the horror of Boredom and the immortal desire to feel themselves living.

By the time my host and I seated ourselves, we were already old, fine friends. We ate, we drank extravagantly all sorts of remarkable wines and, even more remarkable, it seemed to me that after several hours I was no more drunk than he was. But gambling, that superhuman pleasure, had interrupted our drinking at various intervals,

---

1. Baudelaire's allusion to *The Odyssey* borrows some phrasing from Tennyson's "The Lotos-Eaters" (1842).

and I have to say that I bet and lost my soul in a winner-take-all game with a heroic nonchalance and lightheartedness. The soul is such an impalpable thing, so often useless and sometimes so annoying, that its loss made me feel no more emotion than I would have felt if, out for a stroll, I had lost my visiting card.

We slowly smoked cigars whose incomparable savor and scent swept a nostalgia for unknown countries and happinesses into our souls, and drunk with all these delights, in an upsurge of familiarity that did not seem to displease him, I dared to cry out, helping myself to a glass filled to the brim, "to your eternal health, Old Nick!"

We conversed about the universe, from its creation to its future destruction; about this century's great idea, which is to say its belief in progress and perfectibility, and in general about all forms of human infatuation. On that subject, His Highness was not sparing in witty and irrefutable pleasantries, expressing himself with a suavity of diction and a tranquility of humor that I've never encountered in any of humanity's most celebrated conversationalists. He explained to me the absurdity of the different philosophies that have taken possession of the human brain up to the present, and he even deigned to impart a few confidences about some fundamental principles, the possession and benefits of which I choose not to share with just anybody. He did not complain at all about the wicked reputation he had all over the world, assuring me that he himself was the person most interested in the destruction of *superstition*, and he avowed to me that he had only feared once for his power, and that was on the day when he had heard a preacher, more subtle than his colleagues, exclaiming from the pulpit: "My dear brothers, never forget, when you wish to boast about the progress of enlightenment, that the finest of all the devil's tricks was persuading you that he doesn't exist!"

The memory of that celebrated orator led us naturally to the subject of educational institutions, and my strange host asserted to me that he often felt it was not beneath him to inspire the pen, the speech, and the thoughts of pedagogues, and that he was almost always personally present, though invisible, at academic gatherings.

Encouraged by all these kindnesses, I asked him about God and whether he had seen Him recently. He replied in a tone of indifference, but one tinged with a certain sorrow: "We say hello whenever we meet, but it's like the meeting of two old gentlemen who, despite their inborn civility, cannot wholly extinguish the memory of old quarrels."

It is unlikely that His Highness had ever granted so extended an audience to a simple mortal, and I was fearful of abusing it. Finally, as the first glimmers of dawn whitened the windows, this celebrated personage, sung by so many poets and served by so many philosophers who work for his glory without knowing it, said to me: "I want your memory of me to be a pleasant one, and I want to prove to you that I, of whom so many evil things are said, am sometimes a 'good devil,' as one of your popular sayings has it. So, to compensate you for the irremediable loss you've made of your soul, I'll let you have the stakes you would have won if luck had been on your side—that is, the possibility of assuaging and vanquishing, for your entire life, that bizarre disease of Boredom, which is the source of both all your ills and all your miserable progress. You will never form a desire that I won't help you to achieve; you will reign over all your vulgar fellows; you will be furnished with flattery and even adoration; silver, gold, diamonds, fairy palaces will seek you out and beg you to accept them, with no effort on your part to obtain them; you will change your country and nationality as often as you like; you will get yourself drunk with pleasures, never tiring of them, in enchanted lands where it is always warm and where the women smell as fine as flowers—etcetera, etcetera . . . ," he added as he arose, dismissing me with a friendly smile.

If it hadn't been for the fear of humiliating myself before such a grand assembly, I would have willingly thrown myself at the feet of this generous gambler to thank him for his unheard-of munificence. But little by little, after he was gone, that incurable habit of doubt crept back into my breast; I no longer dared to believe in so prodigious a happiness, and when I went to bed, saying my prayers out of a sort of imbecile habit, I repeated, half-asleep: "My God! Oh, my Lord, my God! Make the devil keep his promises to me!"

30

The Rope

For Édouard Manet[1]

*I*llusions," my friend said to me, "may be as innumerable as the varieties of human relationships, or those between people and things. And when the illusion disappears, that is, when we see the creature or the fact as it really is outside of ourselves, we have a bizarre, complex feeling, half regret for the vanished phantom, and half an agreeable surprise at this novelty, at the real fact. Now if there is one phenomenon that is perfectly obvious, ordinary, always the same, one that never fools us, it is maternal love. It is as difficult to imagine a mother without motherly love as it is a light without heat; so, is it not perfectly legitimate to attribute all a mother's acts and words, regarding her child, to maternal love? And yet, listen to this little story, in which I was entirely mystified by this most natural illusion.

"My profession as a painter impels me to look attentively at faces, at the appearances I encounter on my paths, and you know what joy we take from this faculty, which makes life more alive and more meaningful in our eyes than it is for other men. In the remote neighborhood where I live, out where the buildings are still separated by vast grassy spaces, I often used to notice a child whose warm, mischievous expression attracted me at once, more than any others I came across. He posed more than once for me, and I transformed him sometimes into a little Gypsy, sometimes into an angel, sometimes into the mythological Cupid. I made him carry a vagabond's violin, the Crown of Thorns and the Nails of the Passion, and the torch of Eros. Finally, I had come to take such pleasure in the little gamin's pranks that one day I begged his parents, poor people, to let me have him, promising to dress him well, to give him a bit of

---

1. This story is based on a real event. The painter Manet had taken in a local boy named Alexandre, who was the model for his painting *Child with Cherries* (1859), and Alexandre did in fact hang himself in Manet's studio.

money, and never to impose any heavier tasks on him than cleaning my brushes and running my errands. The child, once I had got him cleaned up, became charming, and the life he led with me seemed like a paradise to him, compared to life in his parents' hovel. Only I have to add that the little gentlemen surprised me sometimes with extraordinary, precocious fits of melancholy, and that he soon began to reveal an immoderate taste for sugar and liqueurs; so much so that one day when I confirmed that he had committed yet another theft of this sort, I threatened to send him back to his parents. Then I left, and my business affairs kept me from home for quite a while.

"So you can imagine the horror and shock I felt when, returning home, the first thing I saw was my little gentleman, the mischievous companion of my life, hanging from the panel of that armoire! His feet almost touched the floor; a chair, which he had evidently kicked aside, lay turned over near him; his head hung convulsively on one shoulder; his swollen face and his eyes, wide open in a frightening stare, at first gave me the illusion he was still alive. Taking him down was not as easy a job as you might think. His body was already stiff, and I had an inexplicable horror of letting him fall to the floor. I had to hold him up entirely with one arm, and use the other hand to cut the rope. But then everything was still not done; the little beast had used a thin, tough cord that had cut deeply into the flesh of his neck, and now, with a pair of small scissors, I had to pry out the rope sunk between the rolls of swollen flesh in order to free his neck.

"I forgot to mention that I had called out loudly for help; but all my neighbors refused to come to my aid, in that respect faithful to the customs of civilized humankind who never, I don't know why, want to get mixed up in the affairs of a hanged man. Finally, a doctor came and declared that the child had been dead for several hours. And later, when we had to undress him for the burial, the corpse was so rigid that we were unable to move his limbs, and we had to tear and cut his clothes to get them off.

"The policeman to whom I, of course, had to report the incident glanced at me out of the corner of his eye and said, 'There's something suspicious about all this'—prompted, no doubt, by his stubborn desire and habit of instilling fear in everyone, innocent and guilty alike.

"One supreme task remained, the very thought of which caused me a terrible anguish: I had to notify the parents. My feet refused to take me there. At last I found the courage. But, to my astonishment, the mother was impassive, not even the glint of a tear in her eye. I attributed this strange reaction to the very shock she must have felt, and I remembered the old saying: 'The most terrible griefs are the silent ones.' As for the father, he contented himself with saying, with a half-devastated, half-pensive air: 'After all, perhaps it's for the best; he was never going to turn out well anyway!'

"In the meantime, the body was laid out on my couch and, with a servant's help, I was busy with the final preparations when the mother came into my studio. She wanted, she said, to see the corpse of her son. I really couldn't prevent her from indulging her grief by refusing her this supreme and somber consolation. Then she implored me to show her the place where her little one had hanged himself. 'Oh no, Madame,' I replied; 'that would be too painful for you!' But my eyes involuntarily turned toward the deathly armoire, and I could see, with a mixture of disgust and horror, that the nail was still in the panel, with a long piece of rope still hanging from it. I darted quickly over to tear down these last vestiges of misery, and as I was about to throw them out the open window, the poor woman gripped my arm and said in an irresistible tone: 'Oh, Monsieur! Let me have that! I beg you! Please!' Her despair had evidently, I thought, driven her so mad that she was seized with tenderness for what had been the instrument of her son's death, and wanted to keep it like some horrible and dear relic. And she snatched up the nail and the rope.

"Finally, finally, everything was done. All that remained was for me to get myself back to work, with more intensity than usual, to exorcise that little corpse that still haunted the very folds of my brain, the phantom who wore me down with his large, staring eyes. But the next day I received a stack of letters: some from other inhabitants of my building, some from neighboring houses; one from the first floor, another from the second, another from the third, and so on; some were semi-jocular, as if trying to disguise the eagerness of their request under some light banter, and others entirely shameless and badly spelled, but all of them tending to the same goal, that is, to get a piece of the deathly and beatific rope from me. Among the signatures there were, I must say, more women's than men's, but not all of them, I assure you, were from the lower, vulgar classes. I have kept these letters.

"And then, suddenly, it dawned on me, and I understood why the mother had so insistently snatched the rope from me, and what sort of commerce she had planned for her consolation."[2]

---

2. In the 1864 version, published in *L'Artiste*, Baudelaire included a final paragraph: "'Good heavens,' I replied to my friend: 'One meter of rope from a hanged person, at a hundred francs per decimeter, all in all, with each paying according to his means, that would add up to a thousand francs, a real, effective consolation for the poor mother!'"

31

Vocations

*I*n a beautiful garden where the autumnal sun's rays seemed to be lingering in pleasure, beneath a sky already tinted with green, across which golden clouds floated like drifting continents, four fine children, four boys, apparently tired of play, conversed among themselves.

One was saying: "Yesterday they took me to the theater. There were great, sad palaces behind which you could see the ocean and the sky, and men and women, both serious and sad, but much finer and much better dressed than the ones we see around here, and the way they spoke was like singing. They threatened each other, they begged, they despaired, and they often kept their hand on a dagger stuck in their belt. Oh, it's so beautiful! The women are much more beautiful and taller than the ones who come to visit at our house, and what with their big, hollow eyes and their inflamed cheeks they seemed terrifying, and you couldn't help but love them. Sometimes you're afraid, sometimes you want to cry, but somehow you're happy . . . And then, what's even stranger, it makes you want to dress that way, to say and do the same things, and to speak with that voice . . ."

One of the four children, who for some time had no longer been listening to his comrade's discourse, watching some distant spot in the sky with a strange fixity, suddenly said: "Look, look up there! Do you see that? He's sitting on that little isolated cloud, that fire-colored cloud moving so slowly. *Him* too, it's as if *He's* watching us."

"Who? Who is it?" the others asked.

"God!" he said in a perfectly convinced voice. "Oh! He's already far away; soon you won't be able to see Him. He must be traveling, on His way to visit all the other countries. Wait, He's going to pass beyond that row of trees that's almost at the horizon . . . and now He's sinking behind the church tower . . . Ah, you can't see Him anymore!" And the child stayed turned in that direction for a long time, his eyes fixed on the line separating earth and sky, shining with an ineffable expression of ecstasy and regret.

"He's crazy, that one, with his great God that only he can see," said the third, whose whole little body was expressive of an exceptional vivacity and vitality. "Me, I'm going to tell you about something that happened to me that has never happened to you, and which is a bit more interesting than your theatre and your clouds. —A few days ago, my parents took me on a trip with them and, since the inn we were staying at didn't have enough beds for all of us, it was decided that I would sleep in the same bed with my maid." He motioned his comrades closer to him and spoke more quietly. "This was a strange thing, see, not to be in bed alone and to be in a bed with my maid, in the dark. Since I wasn't sleeping, I amused myself while she slept by running my hand over her arms, her neck, and her shoulders. Her arms and her neck are fatter than any other woman's, and the skin is so soft, so soft, like writing paper or like silk paper. I felt so much pleasure in it that I could have kept on for a long time if I hadn't been afraid, afraid first of waking her, and then of I don't know what. Then I burrowed my face into the hair hanging down her back, thick as a horse's mane, and it smelled as good, I'm telling you, as the flowers in this garden do now. Try, when you get the chance, to do what I did, and you'll see!"

The young author of this prodigious revelation, while telling his story, had his eyes wide with a sort of stupefaction that he still felt, and the rays of the setting sun played over the reddish curls of his tousled hair, lighting it like a sulfurous halo of passion. It was easy to tell that this one would not waste his life in seeking the Divinity in the clouds, and that he would frequently find it elsewhere.

Finally, the fourth one said: "You know that I don't have much fun at my house; they never take me to plays; my tutor is too much of a tightwad; God doesn't occupy Himself with me and my boredom, and I don't have a beautiful maid to pamper me. I've often thought that my greatest pleasure would be just to leave, without knowing where I'm going, and without anyone's worrying about me, and go see new countries all the time. I'm never happy wherever I am, and I always think that I'd be better off anywhere else. So! I saw, at the last fair in the next village, three men who live the way I'd like to live. You didn't notice them, you others. They were big, so dark they were almost black, and very proud even though they were dressed in rags, looking like they had no need of anybody else. Their great, somber eyes suddenly lit up when they made music; a music so startling that it made you feel sometimes like dancing, sometimes like crying, or like doing both at once, and like you'd go mad if you listened to them too long. The one, trailing his bow across his violin, seemed to be describing some sorrow, and the other, bouncing his little hammer over the keyboard strings of a small piano he had hanging from his neck by a strap, seemed to be mocking the other's lament, while the third crashed his cymbals from time to time with an extraordinary violence. They were so happy with each other that they kept on playing their savage music, even after the crowd had dispersed. Finally they gathered up their coins, put their baggage on their backs, and left. Me, I wanted to know where they lived, and I followed them up to the edge of the forest, where I came to understand that they lived nowhere.

"Then one said: 'Should we set up the tent?'

"'No, not at all,' said the other, 'it's such a fine night!'

"The third, counting up the night's take, said, 'These people don't understand music, and their women dance like bears. Fortunately, we'll be in Austria in a month, where we'll find more likeable people.'

"'We might do better to head toward Spain, because the season is getting late; let's avoid the rains, and go where we'll only get our throats wet,' said one of the others.

"I've remembered all of it, as you see. Then they each drank a glass of brandy and went to sleep, lying there facing up at the stars. At first, I wanted to beg them to take me away with them and teach me how to play their instruments; but I didn't dare, I suppose because it's always so hard to make any kind of big decision, and also because I was afraid I'd be caught before we even got out of France."

The lack of interest shown by the three other comrades led me to think that this little one was already one of the *misunderstood*. I watched him attentively; I saw in his eye and in his face that intangible, precociously fatal trait that generally alienates sympathy but which, I don't know why, excited my own, to the point where I suddenly had the bizarre notion that I might have a brother I had never heard about.

The sun went down. Solemn night took possession. The children broke up, each one going, though none of them knew it, to ripen his own destiny according to circumstances and chance, to scandalize his friends, and to gravitate toward glory, or toward dishonor.

32

The Thyrsus

For Franz Liszt[1]

*W*hat is a thyrsus? In the moral and poetic sense, it is a sacerdotal emblem held in the hands of priests or priestesses celebrating the divinity of whom they are the interpreters and servants. But physically it's only a stick, just a stick, like the ones used for supporting vines, dry, stiff, and straight. Around the stick are wound stems and flowers that seem to meander capriciously, playing, frolicking, some sinuous and fugitive, some hanging down like bells or upside-down cups. And a stunning glory springs from this complexity of line and color, sometimes tender, sometimes bold. Doesn't it seem as if the curved line and the spiral are paying court to the straight line, dancing around it in mute adoration? Doesn't it seem as if all these delicate corollas, all these calyxes, exploding with scent and color, are performing a mystical fandango around the hieratic stick? And yet, who is the impudent mortal who would dare to decide whether the flowers and tendrils were made for the stick, or whether the stick is only the pretext for revealing the beauty of the flowers and tendrils? The thyrsus is the representation of your startling duality, powerful and venerated master, dear Bacchant of mysterious and passionate Beauty. No nymph inflamed by the invisible Bacchus ever shook her thyrsus over the heads of her maddened companions with as much energy and caprice as you, when you work your genius on the hearts of your brothers.—The stick is your will, straight, strong and invincible; the flowers are the winding strollings of your fantasy around your will; they are the feminine element performing its dazzling pirouettes around the male. The straight line, the arabesque line, intention and expression, the straightness of the will, the sinuousness of the word, united toward

---

1. Liszt and Baudelaire admired each other's work. Liszt had sent Baudelaire a copy of his *The Gypsies and Their Music in Hungary* (1859), and Baudelaire had sent him a copy of his *Artificial Paradises*.

one goal with varying means, the all-powerful and indivisible amalgam of genius: What analyst would have the detestable courage to divide and separate you?

Dear Liszt, through the mists, beyond the rivers, above the towns where the pianos sing your glory, where the printing presses translate your wisdom, in whatever land you are, whether in the splendors of the eternal city or in the mists of the dreaming countries that Cambrinus[2] consoles, improvising your songs of delectation or of ineffable sorrow, or confiding your abstruse meditations to paper, singer of eternal Delight and Anguish, philosopher, poet, and artist, I salute you in your immortality!

---

2. The semi-mythical "king of beer" or inventor of beer, mentioned in many student songs in Germany and Belgium.

33

Get Yourself Drunk

*Y*ou should always be drunk. This is the whole point, the only question. In order not to feel the horrible burden of Time that breaks your shoulders and bends you down toward the ground, you must get yourself relentlessly drunk.

But drunk on what? On wine, on poetry, or on virtue, whatever you like. But get yourself drunk.

And if at some point, on the steps of a palace or on the green grass of a ditch or in the sad solitude of your room, you awaken with your drunkenness already diminished or vanished, ask the wind, the wave, the star, the bird, the clock, everything that flees, everything that groans, everything that rolls, everything that sighs, everything that speaks, ask them what time it is, and the wind, the wave, the star, the bird, the clock will reply: "It's time to get drunk! So as not to be one of the martyred slaves of Time, get yourself drunk; get yourself drunk always! On wine, on poetry, or on virtue, whatever you like."

34

Already!

A hundred times already the sun had sprung, radiant or darkened, from the immense tub of the sea whose borders could scarcely be perceived; a hundred times it had plunged back, sparkling or morose, into its evening bath. For many days we had been able to contemplate the other side of the firmament and decipher the celestial alphabet of the antipodes. And each of the passengers moaned and groaned. It was as if the approach of land worsened their suffering. "When, when," they said, "will we stop sleeping a sleep tossed by the waves, troubled by a wind whose snoring is louder than ours? When will we be able to eat meat that isn't as salted as this cursed element that carries us? When will we be able to digest our food sitting in a stable easy chair?"

Among them were some who thought of their hearths, who missed their unfaithful, sullen wives and their shrieking offspring. All were so maddened by the absent land that I believe they would have eaten grass with more enthusiasm than the animals do.

Finally, a shore was sighted; and as we approached, we saw that it was a magnificent, dazzling land. It seemed as if the varied musics of life emanated from it in a vague murmur, and that its coasts, rich in every shade of green, exhaled in all directions a delicious odor of flowers and fruits.

Suddenly everyone was joyous, each abdicated his state of bad humor. All quarrels were forgotten, all reciprocal wrongs were forgiven; the duels that had been arranged were erased from memory, and all the grudges evaporated like smoke.

I alone was sad, inconceivably sad. Like a priest whose god has been wrenched away from him, I could not detach myself, without a heartrending bitterness, from that sea so monstrously seductive, that sea so infinitely varied in its terrifying simplicity, that sea that seemed to contain within itself and represent by its tricks, its allurements, its rages and its smiles, the temperaments, the agonies and ecstasies of every soul that ever lived, lives, or will live!

In saying goodbye to that incomparable beauty, I felt myself beaten down almost to death; and that is why, when each of my companions said, "Finally!" I could only cry, "Already!"

And yet this was the earth, the earth with its noises, its passions, its commodities and its festivals; it was a rich and magnificent earth, filled with promises, sending up to us a mysterious perfume of roses and musk, along with the varied musics of life in an amorous murmur.

Windows

A person who stands outside gazing through an open window never sees as many things as the one who gazes at a closed one. There is no object more profound, more mysterious, more fecund, more shadowy, more dazzling than a window lit by a candle. What can be seen in broad daylight is always less interesting than what happens behind a window. Within that black or illuminated hole, life lives, life dreams, life suffers.

Beyond the waves of rooftops, I see a mature woman, one already wrinkled, poor, always bent over something, never going outside—and by using her face, using her clothes, using her gestures, with almost no materials, I have recreated this woman's history, or her legend, rather, and sometimes I narrate it to myself, in tears.

If it had been a poor old man, I would have recreated his just as easily.

And I go to bed, proud of having lived and suffered in people other than myself.

Perhaps you will ask, "Are you sure that this legend is true?" But what does it matter, the reality situated outside of me, if it helps me to feel that I am and what I am?

The Desire to Paint

*M*iserable the man may be, but happy is the artist torn by desire!

I burn to paint the one who so rarely appeared to me, who so quickly fled from me, like a beautiful, regrettable thing that the traveler, carried off by the night, leaves behind him. How long already since she disappeared!

She is beautiful, and more than beautiful: she is surprising. The dark abounds in her: and everything she inspires is nocturnal and profound. Her eyes are two lairs where mystery vaguely flickers, and her gaze illuminates like lightning: an explosion in the shadows.

I would compare her to a black sun, if one could imagine a black star that sheds light and happiness. But she makes me think more easily of the moon, which has certainly marked her with its formidable influence; not the white moon of the idylls, so like a cold wife, but the sinister, intoxicating moon, suspended in the depths of a storm-filled night, a night jostled by the racing clouds; not the peaceable, discreet moon that visits the dreams of pure men, but the moon ripped from the sky, vanquished and rebellious, that the Thessalian witches grimly forced to dance on the terrified grass![1]

Behind her small brow, a tenacious will and the love of prey reside. However, toward the bottom of this disquieting face, near the always mobile nostrils breathing in the unknown and the impossible, there flashes out with inexpressible grace the smile of a wide mouth, red and white, and delicious, which makes one dream of the miracle of a superb flower blossoming on volcanic terrain.

There are women who inspire in us the wish to conquer and to use them; but this one arouses the desire to die, slowly, beneath her gaze.

---

1. Baudelaire alludes here to Lucan's (39–65 CE) epic poem on the Roman civil war, known as the *Pharsalia* (the Thessalian witches figure in Book VI). Lucan's taste for the bizarre and the demonic always appealed to Baudelaire, who thought modern critics undervalued him; in one of his lists of titles for an expanded *Paris Spleen,* he included the title "The Last Songs of Lucan."

The Favors of the Moon[1]

*T*he Moon, the very embodiment of caprice, looked through the window while you slept in your cradle, and said: "I like this child."

And soft as fleece, she descended her stairway of clouds, passing soundlessly through the window. Then she stretched herself out across you with a mother's pliant tenderness, leaving her colors upon your face. This is why the pupils of your eyes are green, and your cheeks so extraordinarily pale. And it was by contemplating this visitor that your eyes became so bizarrely enlarged; and so tenderly did she embrace your throat, that ever since you have felt like weeping.

However, in her expansive joy, the Moon filled the whole room like a phosphoric atmosphere, like a luminous poison; and this living light thought, and it said: "You will forever submit to the influence of my kiss. Your beauty will be like mine. You will love what I love, and whatever loves me: water, clouds, silence, and night; the immense green sea; water both formless and multiform; the place where you are not; the lover you do not know; monstrous flowers; perfumes inducing delirium; languorous cats lying on pianos, moaning like women in husky, sweet voices!

"And you will be loved by my lovers, courted by those who court me. You will be the queen of green-eyed men whose throats I have also embraced in my nocturnal caresses; of those who love the sea, the immense, tumultuous and green sea, the formless and multiform water, the places they are not, the women they do not know, the sinister flowers like the censers of an unknown religion, the perfumes

---

1. In its original version, this poem was dedicated to "Mademoiselle B.," that is, to Berthe, a woman with whom Baudelaire had a relationship during the years 1863–1864. Little is known about her, but she was probably an actress, and she is probably also the woman in "The Soup and the Clouds" (number 44), from which we can glimpse something of her temperament—and her appeal to Baudelaire.

that trouble the will, and the wild, sensual animals that are the emblems of their madness."

And that is why, my cursed, dear, spoiled child, I now lie at your feet, seeking in every part of you the reflection of the fearful Divinity, the lethal godmother, the poisonous nurse of all the *lunatics.*

38

Which Is the Real One?

I knew a certain Benedicta, who radiated the ideal, whose eyes sowed the seeds of the desire for greatness, for beauty, for fame, and for everything that makes us believe in immortality.

But this miraculous girl was too beautiful to live very long; thus she died only a few days after I met her, and I myself buried her, on a day when spring swung its censer even in the graveyards. I myself buried her, sealed up in a coffin of perfumed and incorruptible wood, like a chest from India.

And while my eyes remained fixed on the place to which my treasure had fled, I suddenly saw a small woman who strongly resembled the departed one, and who, pawing the fresh earth with hysterical, bizarre violence, broke into laughter and said: "It's me, the real Benedicta! It's me, a celebrated slut! And as punishment for your madness and your blindness, you will love me just as I am!"

But I, furious, replied "No! No! No!" And to give greater emphasis to my rejection, I stamped my foot so violently on the earth that my leg sank up to the knee in the fresh grave, and like a wolf caught in a trap, I remain, perhaps forever, attached to the grave of the ideal.

A Thoroughbred

She's certainly ugly. But she's delicious nonetheless! Time and Love have scarred her with their claws and have taught her cruelly just how much each minute and each kiss reduces her youth and her freshness.

She is truly ugly; ant-like, spider-like, even skeleton-like if you prefer; but she is also a potion, *magic,* sorcery! In short, she is exquisite.

Time could not break down the lively harmony of her gait nor the indestructible elegance of her frame. Love has not altered the sweetness of her childlike breath; and Time has taken nothing away from her abundant mane, which still exhales, in musky scents, all the wild vitality of the South of France: Nimes, Aix, Arles, Avignon, Narbonne, Toulouse, blessed cities of the sun, of passion and enchantment!

Time and Love have gnawed away at her vigorously but in vain; they have diminished nothing of the vague but eternal charm of her boyish chest.

Worn down perhaps but not worn out, and forever heroic, she makes you think of those nobly-descended thoroughbreds that the real connoisseur can always recognize, even when hitched up to a coach for hire or to a clumsy cart.

And then she is so sweet-natured and so fervent! She loves the way one loves in Autumn; it's as if the approach of winter has lit a new fire in her heart, and the servility in her tenderness is never tiresome.

40

The Mirror

A hideous man comes in and gazes at himself in the mirror.

"Why do you look at yourself in the mirror, when you can't possibly see yourself without displeasure?"

The hideous man replies to me: "Monsieur, according to the immortal principles of 1789,[1] all men have equal rights; therefore I have the right to look in the mirror; whether with pleasure or displeasure is nobody's business but mine."

In terms of good sense, I was certainly right; but, from the point of view of the law, he was not wrong.

---

1. That is, the principles associated with the French Revolution—liberty, equality, fraternity.

The Port

A port is a charming resting place for the soul wearied by the struggles of life. The breadth of the sky, the moving architecture of the clouds, the changing colorations of the sea, the twinkling of the lighthouses are a prism marvelously well suited for amusing the eyes without ever tiring them. The darting shapes of the ships, with their complicated rigging, which trace the harmonious oscillations of the ocean swells, help maintain the soul's taste for rhythm and beauty. And, above all, there is a kind of mysterious, aristocratic pleasure for those who no longer have any curiosity or ambition, to contemplate, while lying in the summerhouse or leaning on the pier, all the movements of those who depart and those who return, of those who still have the strength to want anything, the desire to travel or to get rich.

Portraits of Mistresses

*I*n a male version of a boudoir—that is, a smoking room adjoining an elegant gambling house—four men sat smoking and talking. They were not exactly young or old, neither handsome nor ugly; but young or old, they bore that unmistakable mark of veterans of pleasure, that indescribable something, that cold and scoffing melancholy that plainly declared: "We have lived fully, and we are in search of something we can love and admire."

One of them turned the discussion toward the topic of women. It would have been more philosophical not to speak of them at all; but there are some clever enough men who, after some drinking, will not scorn a banal conversation. In such situations, one listens to the man speaking as one would listen to dance music.

"Every man," he was saying, "has had his Chérubin[1] period: it's the time when, for lack of a dryad, one willingly embraces the trunk of an oak. This is the first stage of love. In the second stage, one becomes more selective. The ability to deliberate is already a decadence. This is when one determinedly seeks out beauty. But for me, my friends, I am proud of having arrived at last at the climacteric period, the third stage, where beauty itself is not enough unless it is seasoned with perfume, fine clothes, etcetera. And I'll admit that I aspire sometimes, as to an unknown bliss, to reach a certain fourth stage, which must be defined as absolute calm. But throughout my life, with the exception of the Chérubin stage, I was more aware than anyone else of the annoying stupidity, the irritating mediocrity of women. What I like best about animals is their candor. So consider, then, how much my last mistress has made me suffer.

"She was the bastard offspring of a prince. Beautiful, certainly; otherwise, why would I have taken her on? But she spoiled that great quality by an indecorous and deformed ambition. This was a woman who always wanted to play the man: 'You're no man! Ah, if I were a man! Of the two of us, I'm the one who's the man!' Such

---

1. The young page in Beaumarchais' *Marriage of Figaro* (1781).

were the intolerable refrains coming out of that mouth from which I only wanted to hear songs taking flight. And if I let my admiration for a book, a poem, an opera escape my lips, she would immediately say: 'Do you really think that's good? But then, what do you know about greatness?' And she would start in arguing.

"One fine day, she decided to take up chemistry; and from then on, there was always a glass mask between my lips and hers. And along with all that, a strong prudery. If now and then I upset her by making a slightly over-amorous move, she convulsed like a violated flower . . ."

"How did it end?" asked one of the others. "I've never known you to be so patient."

"God," he replied, "sends the cure along with the disease. One day I discovered my Minerva, starved by her powerful ideal, in a compromising situation with my servant, a situation obliging me to retire discreetly so as not to cause them to blush. That evening I dismissed them both, paying them their back wages."

"As for me," said the one who had interrupted, "I've never had anyone to complain about but myself. Happiness came to live with me, and I didn't recognize it. Not long ago, fate granted me the joy of a woman who was the sweetest, the most submissive, and the most devoted of creatures, and always ready! And without enthusiasm! 'I'm happy to do it, since it pleases you.' That was her usual response. You could pound on that wall or this couch, and you'd get more sighs out of them than ever escaped from the lips of my mistress, even during the wildest bouts of lovemaking. After we had lived together for a year, she admitted to me that she had never known pleasure. I grew tired of that one-sided duel, and the incomparable girl got married. Later, I gave in to a whim to see her again, and she showed me her six beautiful children, saying, 'Well, my dear friend! The wife is just as much a *virgin* as the mistress was.' Nothing about her had changed. Sometimes, I regret it; I should have married her."

The others all laughed, and the third one said in his turn:

"My friends, I have known some pleasures that you have perhaps neglected. I want to talk about comedy in love, a comedy that even inspires admiration. I admired my last mistress more, I think, than you could have hated or loved yours. And everyone else admired her just as much. Whenever we entered a restaurant, after a few moments everyone forgot about eating and contemplated only her. Even the waiters and the women at the counter felt the effects of that contagious ecstasy of hers and neglected their duties. In short, I lived for a while on intimate terms with a living *freak*. She ate, chewed, gnawed, devoured, and swallowed, but in the lightest, most carefree way in the world. She kept me in ecstasy for a very long time. She would say, 'I'm hungry,' in a sweet, dreamy, English, romantic way. And revealing the prettiest teeth in the world, she would repeat the words day and night—you would have been moved and amused at the same time.—I could have made my fortune by exhibiting her at fairs as an *omnivorous monster*. I nourished her well; but still she left me . . ."

"For a grocer, no doubt?"

"Something like that, a kind of clerk in the military supply commission who, by some sort of magic wand he had, could perhaps arrange to give the poor girl the rations of several soldiers. At least that's what I thought."

"As for me," the fourth one said, "I've endured atrocious suffering from the opposite of what's usually called female egoism. I think you're sadly mistaken, you too-fortunate mortals, to complain of your mistresses' imperfections!"

This was said in a very serious tone by a man who seemed gentle and composed, with an almost clerical look about him, his face illuminated by clear, grey eyes whose gaze seemed to say: "I want this!" or, "You must do that!" or even, "I never forgive!"

"If, excitable as I know you to be, G, or slack and feeble as you two, K and J, if you had been coupled with a certain woman I know, either you would have run away or you'd have ended up dead. Me, I survived, as you see. Imagine a woman incapable of making an error either in feeling or in judgment; a woman with a disturbingly calm character, devotion without comedy or pomposity, sweetness without frailty, energy without violence. The story of my love affair is like an endless voyage over a surface pure and polished as a mirror, dizzyingly monotonous, which reflected all my own feelings and gestures with the ironic precision of my own conscience, so that I could not allow myself any unreasonable sentiment or action without feeling the immediate reproach of my inseparable specter. Love seemed to me like a tutoring session. How many stupid things she prevented me from doing, things I regret not doing! How many debts she made me pay in spite of myself! She deprived me of any benefits that I might have drawn from my personal folly. With cold, unbreakable rules, she thwarted all my whims. And what's worst of all, she never insisted I thank her when the danger had passed! How many times did I have to stop myself from grabbing her by the throat and shouting: 'Be a little imperfect, you miserable woman! So that I can love you without feeling sick and furious!' I admired her for several years, my heart full of hatred. But in the end, I'm not the one who's dead!"

"Ah," said the others, "so she's dead?"

"Yes! It couldn't go on like that. Love had become an overwhelming nightmare for me. Victory or death, as the politicians say, this was the choice my destiny had given me. One night, in a wood . . . beside a pond . . . after a melancholy walk in which her eyes reflected all the sweetness of the heavens, and my nerves were at the breaking point . . ."

"What!"

"What do you mean!"

"What are you saying?"

"It was inevitable. I had too much of a sense of fairness to beat, insult, or dismiss such an irreproachable servant. But I had to balance that sense together with the horror the creature inspired in me; to get rid of the creature without showing any disrespect. What else could I do with her, *since she was perfect?*"

His three friends looked at him with a vaguely stupefied expression, as if pretending not to understand and as if implicitly avowing that, as far as they were concerned, they did not feel themselves capable of so harsh an act, no matter how convincingly explained it had been.

Then they called for another round, to kill the Time that grips life so mercilessly, and to accelerate the monotonous stream of Life.

43

The Gallant Marksman

*A*s the coach passed through the forest, he ordered the driver to stop near a firing range, saying that he would enjoy the chance to fire a few rounds just to *kill* time. And killing that monster—isn't this everyone's most ordinary and legitimate occupation?—And he offered his hand gallantly to his dear, delicious, and detestable woman, the mysterious wife to whom he owed so many pleasures, so many sorrows, and perhaps a considerable part of his genius as well.

Several bullets struck far from their intended target; one of them even ended up embedded in the ceiling; and when the charming creature laughed wildly, mocking the ineptitude of her spouse, he turned abruptly toward her and said: "Look at that doll over there on the right, the one with her nose in the air and a haughty look about her. Well! My dear angel, *I'm going to imagine that it's you.*" He closed his eyes and pulled the trigger. The doll was neatly decapitated.

Then bending toward his dear, his delicious, his detestable wife, his inevitable and pitiless Muse, and kissing her hand respectfully, he added: "Ah, my dear angel, I thank you so much for my skill!"

44

The Soup and the Clouds

*M*y beloved little maniac was making me dinner, and from the open window of the dining room I contemplated the drifting architectures that God makes out of vapors, those marvelous constructions of the impalpable. And in my contemplation, I was saying to myself: "All these phantasmal clouds are almost as beautiful as the eyes of my beautiful beloved, my darling monstrous little green-eyed maniac."

And suddenly I felt a violent punch in my back, and I heard a husky, charming voice, a hysterical voice hoarsened by brandy, the voice of my dear little beloved, who was saying: "So are you going to eat your soup, you son of a bitch of a cloud merchant?"

45

The Firing Range and the Graveyard

T$he Graveyard View Tavern.*[1]—"An extraordinary signboard,"
said our stroller to himself, "but well designed to make one
thirsty! Surely the tavern owner is one who appreciates Horace
and the poets who were disciples of Epicurus. Perhaps he is also
familiar with the profound refinements of the ancient Egyptians, for
whom no fine banquet was complete without a skeleton, or some
other emblem of the brevity of life."

And he went in, drank a glass of beer facing the tombs, and
slowly smoked a cigar. On a sudden whim he decided to go down to
the cemetery, for the grass was tall and inviting, and a rich sun
reigned over all.

In fact, the raging light and heat seemed to emanate from a
drunken sun, which sprawled at full length on a carpet of magnifi-
cent flowers fattened by the decay beneath. An immense murmur-
ing of life filled the air—the life of the infinitesimally small—
broken at regular intervals by the crackle of rifle shots from a neigh-
boring firing range, which popped like champagne corks amid
a humming, muted symphony.

Then, under the sun that was burning his brain, and in the
atmosphere of Death's hot perfumes, he heard a voice whispering
from under the tomb on which he sat. And the voice said: "Accursed
be your targets and your carbines, you restless living ones, since you
have so little respect for the deceased and their holy place of repose!
Accursed be your ambitions, accursed be your schemes, you
impatient mortals, who come to study the art of killing so near to
the sanctuary of Death! If you only knew how easy it is to win this
prize, how easy it is to hit this target, and how everything is
nothingness except for Death, you would not exhaust yourselves so,
you laborious living ones, and you would trouble less often the sleep
of those who have long ago hit the Target, the only real target of
this detestable life!"

1. Baudelaire had encountered a tavern with this name in the countryside outside
Brussels.

46

Loss of a Halo

*W*hat? You here, my dear friend? You, in a nasty place like this! You, the drinker of quintessences, the eater of ambrosia! Really, this is quite a surprise."

"My friend, you know my horror of horses and carriages. Just now, as I was crossing the boulevard in a great hurry, hopping over the mud in that moving chaos where death gallops down on you from all sides at once, I made a sudden brusque movement and my halo slipped from my head, down onto the muddy street. It wasn't worth the trouble going back for it. I felt it would be less unpleasant to lose my badge than to break my bones. And then, I told myself, every bad thing has its good side. Now I can walk about incognito, do vile things, and give myself up to debauchery, like simple mortals. And here I am, looking just like you, as you see!"

"You ought to at least put up a notice about the halo, or have the police help you retrieve it."

"Good heavens, no! I like it fine here. You're the only one to have recognized me. And besides, dignity bores me. And I love to think that some fool poet will pick it up and shamelessly put it on. Making someone happy—what a pleasure! And even better, when it's someone you can laugh at! Imagine it on X, or on Z! Eh? Wouldn't that be a laugh?"

47

Mademoiselle Bistouri[1]

*A*s I was walking under the gas lamps near the outer edge of town, I felt an arm slip gently under mine, and I heard a voice close to my ear saying: "You are a doctor, monsieur?"

I looked; it was a tall, robust girl with wide eyes, her face lightly made up, her hair lifted by the wind along with the ribbons of her bonnet.

"No, I am not a doctor. Let me be."

"Oh yes! You *are* a doctor. I can tell. Come to my house. You'll be very pleased with me; come on!"

"Maybe I will come visit you, but *after the doctor,* damn it!"

"Ah, ah," she said, continuing to hang on to my arm, and beginning to laugh, "You're a comical doctor. I've known quite a few like you! Come on."

I dearly love a mystery, because I always hope I'll be able to solve it. So I let myself be pulled along by this new companion, or rather by this unexpected enigma.

I omit any description of her hovel; it can be found in many of the old, well-known French poets. However, in a detail that Régnier[2] missed, two or three portraits of famous doctors hung on the walls.

How pampered I was! A large fire, mulled wine, cigars; and while offering me these fine things and lighting a cigar herself, the ludicrous creature said to me: "Make yourself at home, my friend, make yourself comfortable. This will all remind you of the hospital and of the good old days of your youth.—Oh my! How did your hair get so white? It wasn't like that then, such a long time ago, when you were an intern under L. I remember you were the one who assisted him in serious operations. Now there was a man who loved to cut,

---

1. A "bistouri" is a lancet or surgical knife. This poem, now recognized as one of Baudelaire's greatest, was at first accepted by the *Revue nationale et étrangère* in 1867, but ultimately was rejected as unpublishable.

2. Mathurin Régnier (1573–1613), one of French literature's greatest satirists.

and prune and lop! You were the one who handed the instruments to him, the sutures and the sponges.—And I remember how, when the operation was done, he would consult his watch and proudly declare, 'Five minutes, gentlemen!'—Oh, me, I get around. I know all those gentlemen well."

A few seconds later, speaking more familiarly now, she picked up her tale again, saying, "You're a doctor, aren't you, my little tiger?"

This insane refrain of hers made me jump up out of the chair. "No!" I cried furiously.

"A surgeon, then?"

"No, no! Unless I'm surgeon enough to cut off your head! Sacred ciborium of a holy mackerel!"[3]

"Wait," she replied. "You'll see."

And she took a bundle of papers out of an armoire, which turned out to be the collection of celebrated doctors' portraits, lithographed by Maurin,[4] which had been displayed for some years on the Quai Voltaire.

"Look! Do you recognize him?"

"Yes! It's X. His name is printed below the picture; but I happen to know him personally."

"Of course you do! Here, look at Z, the man who described X in a lecture as 'the monster who reveals the blackness of his soul on his face!' And all that just because the two of them didn't agree on a particular case! How everyone at the University laughed, back then Do you remember?—Here, look at K, the one who informed on the insurgents he was treating at his hospital. That was during the riots.[5] How could so fine a man have so little courage?—And here's W, a famous English doctor; I got hold of him during his trip to Paris. He almost looks like a girl, doesn't he?"

---

3. The comical, exasperated curse was presented only in its initials in the printed text, inviting the reader to fill in the semi-blasphemous words, but it is spelled out in Baudelaire's manuscript.

4. Antoine Maurin (1793–1860), a French painter and lithographer who produced many portraits of contemporaries.

5. The reference is to the uprisings of June 1848.

And when I put my hand on a packet tied with string that was lying on the table, she said: "Wait a bit; that one is the interns, and this packet is the nonresidents."

And she then fanned out a stack of photographs, representing much younger faces.

"When we meet again, you'll give me your picture, won't you, dear?"

"But," I said to her, unable to shake free of my own personal obsession, "why do you believe I'm a doctor?"

"Because you're so nice, and so good to women!"

"Strange logic!" I said to myself.

"Oh, I'm hardly ever wrong; I've known so many of them. I love these gentlemen so much that, even though I'm not sick, I sometimes go to them just to see them. Some of them say coldly: 'You are not at all ill!' But some of them understand me, when they see how I smile at them."

"And when they don't understand you?"

"Heavens! Since I've bothered them for *nothing,* I leave ten francs on the mantel.—They're so good and so sweet, those men! —I discovered a little intern at the Pitié, pretty as an angel and so polite! And how hard he works, the poor boy! His friends told me that he didn't have a cent, because his parents are poor and can't send him anything. That gave me confidence. After all, I'm pretty enough, though not so young. I said to him: 'Come see me, come see me often. And with me, don't worry: I don't need any money!' But you understand that I had to get that across in a variety of ways; I couldn't just say it crudely. I was so afraid of humiliating him, the dear child!

"Well! Would you believe that I had a funny kind of urge that I didn't dare tell him?—I wanted him to come see me with his medical bag and his operating smock, even with a bit of blood on it!"

She said this quite candidly, the way a man of the world might say to an actress he was in love with, "I want to see you dressed in the costume you wore in your famous role."

I stubbornly persisted in questioning her: "Can you recall when and where this strange passion of yours began?"

I had a hard time making myself understood; finally I succeeded. But then she replied in a deeply sad tone, even, as near as I can recall, turning her eyes away from me: "I don't know . . . I don't remember."

What bizarre things can be found in a large city, when one knows how to walk around and look for them! Life swarms with innocent monsters.—O Lord, my God! You the Creator, you the Master; you who have made both Law and Liberty; you the sovereign who permits, you the judge who pardons; you who are filled with motives and causes, and who have perhaps put the taste for horror in my spirit in order to convert my heart, like the healing that comes from the tip of a knife blade; Lord, have pity, have pity on the madmen and madwomen! O, Creator! Can they seem to be monsters in the eyes of you who alone know why they exist, how they *were made* and how they *might have been made otherwise?*

48

Any Where Out of the World[1]

*T*his life is a hospital where each patient is obsessed with switching beds. This one wants to go suffer facing the stove, and that one thinks he'll get better if he's next to the window.

It always seems to me that I would be better off in any place but the one where I am, and this question of moving on is one I endlessly discuss with my soul.

"Tell me, my soul, my poor cold soul, what would you think of living in Lisbon? It must be warm there, and you would cheer up there like a lizard. The city is on the water's edge; they say it's built of marble, and that the people there have such a hatred for vegetation that they cut down all the trees. Now there's a country to your taste: a landscape made of light and of mineral, and liquid to reflect them!"

My soul does not respond.

"Since you have such a love of repose and of watching the spectacle of movement, would you like to go live in Holland, that enchanting land? Perhaps you would be entertained in that country whose image you've so often admired in museums. What would you think of Rotterdam, you who love forests of masts, and boats moored outside houses?"

My soul remains mute.

"Would Batavia make you smile more? We would find there the European spirit wedded with tropical beauty."

Not a word.—Is my soul dead?

"So, have you become so benumbed that you'll only take pleasure in your own disease? If that's the way it is, let's flee to those countries that resemble Death.—I know what you need, poor soul! We'll

---

1. The title, spelled thus and appearing in English in the original, comes from Thomas Hood's (1799–1845) poem "The Bridge of Sighs"; Baudelaire translated it in 1865. Hood's poem concerns a woman deceived by her lover and rejected by her family; she kills herself by throwing herself into a river, not caring where the stream takes her so long as it is "anywhere out of the world." The title and its associations create a powerful link between this poem and the preceding one.

pack up our trunks for Torneo. We'll go even farther, to the extreme end of the Baltic; even farther from life, if that's possible; we'll set up house at the Pole. There, the sun only nears the earth obliquely, and the slow alterations of light and night suppress variety and augment monotony, that other kind of nothingness. There, we can take long baths of shadows, except when, from time to time, the Northern Lights will entertain us with their pink sprays, like a reflection of Hell's fireworks!"

At last, my wise soul bursts out and cries: "Anywhere! Anywhere! As long as it's out of this world!"

49

Let's Beat Up the Poor!

*F*or a couple of weeks I was confined to my room, and I surrounded myself with some of the books that were in fashion then (this was sixteen or seventeen years ago);[1] I mean the kind of books that expound upon the art of making the masses happy, wise, and rich, in twenty-four hours. I thus digested—or swallowed, I should say—all the lucubrations of all those entrepreneurs of public happiness—from those who advised that the poor should all become slaves, to those who tried to persuade them that they were all dethroned royalty.—It won't be surprising to learn, then, that I was in a vertiginous state bordering on idiocy.

Yet it seemed to me that I sensed, buried somewhere in the depths of my intellect, the obscure germ of an idea that was superior to the whole dictionary of old wives' formulas that I had just read through. But it was only the idea of an idea, something infinitely vague.

And I went out enormously thirsty. Because an impassioned taste for bad reading engenders a proportionate need for open air and cool drinks.

As I was about to enter a tavern, a beggar held out his hat to me, with one of those unforgettable gazes that could overturn thrones—if mind could move matter, or if the hypnotist's eye could ripen grapes.[2]

At the same time, I heard a voice whispering at my ear, a voice I recognized perfectly well; it was the voice of the good Angel, or good Demon, who always accompanies me. Since Socrates had his good Demon, why shouldn't I have my good Angel, and why shouldn't I, like Socrates, have the honor of obtaining my own certificate of insanity, signed by the subtle Lélut and the sagacious Baillarger?[3]

---

1. This would place the incident in the revolutionary era of 1848.

2. There were in fact experiments in the nineteenth century to hasten the ripening of grapes through hypnotism.

3. L. F. Lélut and Jules-Gabriel-François Baillarger were celebrated psychologists who argued that Socrates' claim to hear an admonishing voice showed clear signs of incipient insanity.

There is one difference between Socrates' Demon and mine: his only manifested itself to him in order to forbid, to warn, to prevent, while mine condescends to counsel, to suggest, to persuade. Poor Socrates only had a prohibiting Demon; mine is a great affirmer, a Demon of action, a Demon of combat.

Now, my Demon whispered to me: "The only man who is the equal of another is the one who proves it, and the only man who is worthy of liberty is the man who knows how to take it."

Immediately, I jumped on the beggar. With one punch I blackened one of his eyes, which in a second swelled up like a ball. I broke one of my fingernails in knocking out two of his teeth, and since I've never felt I was strong enough, having been born delicate and not having had much boxing experience, in order to overpower the old man quickly I grabbed him by the collar with one hand while grasping him around the throat with the other, and I set about banging his head vigorously against a wall. I must admit that before all this I had cast a quick glance around the area, and that I had verified that in this empty suburb where I found myself I would be safe for quite a while from any policemen.

Then, having knocked the weakened sixty-year-old to the ground, I gave him a swift kick to the back, strong enough to break his spine, seized a thick tree branch that hung close to the ground, and beat him with the stubborn energy of a chef tenderizing a beefsteak.

Suddenly—O, miracle! O, joy of the philosopher verifying the excellence of his theory!—I saw this antique carcass turn itself around, and attack me with an energy that I would never have suspected in such a broken-down machine; and, with a look of hatred that seemed to me to *augur well,* the decrepit old rogue threw himself on me, blackened both my eyes, knocked out four of my teeth, and with the same tree branch beat me flatter than plaster.— With my strong medicine, I had thus given him back both his pride and his life.

Then, I made vigorous signs to lead him to understand that I considered our discussion concluded, and pulling myself to my feet with all the satisfaction of a sophist of the Portico, I said to him: "Monsieur, *you are my equal!* Do me the honor of sharing my purse; and remember, if you are a true philanthropist, whenever one of your colleagues asks you for alms, you must apply to them the same theory that I took pains to try out on your back."

He assured me that he understood my theory, and that he would follow my advice.

50

Good Dogs

For Joseph Stevens[1]

I have never felt ashamed of expressing my admiration for Buffon,[2] even among the young writers of my century; but nowadays, it is not the soul of that painter of nature in all its grandeur that I would invoke to aid me. No.

I would much more willingly call upon Sterne, and I would say to him: "Descend from the heavens, or rise toward me from the Elysian Fields to inspire me to sing of good dogs, of poor dogs, a song worthy of you, you sentimental jokester, you incomparable jokester! Return astride that famous ass that always accompanies you in posterity's memory; and above all, do not let the ass forget to carry, suspended daintily between his lips, his immortal macaroon!"[3]

Away with the academic muse! I want nothing to do with that old prude. I invoke the familiar muse, the city girl, the lively one, for her to help me sing of good dogs, poor dogs, stinking dogs, the ones that everyone shoos away as if pestilent and flea-bitten, except for the poor whose companions they are, and the poet who regards them with a brotherly eye.

Away with the dandified dog, with the fatuous quadruped, the Great Dane, the King Charles, the pug, or the Spaniel, so enamored of himself that he leaps indiscreetly against the legs or into the lap of the visitor as if he were sure to be liked, noisy as a child, stupid as a streetwalker, surly and insolent as a servant! And away above all with those four-pawed serpents, shuddering and indolent, named

---

1. Joseph Stevens (1816–1892) was a painter who befriended Baudelaire in Belgium. His works featured animals, especially dogs, and one painting in particular, *L'Intérieur du saltimbanque,* clearly inspired this poem.

2. George-Louis Leclerc, Comte de Buffon (1707–1788) wrote voluminously on, among many other things, animal life.

3. The incident of the ass and the macaroon is in Laurence Sterne's *Tristram Shandy* (1760), Book VII, Chapter XXXII.

greyhounds, whose pointed muzzles don't have enough sense of smell to follow the trail of a friend, whose flattened heads don't have enough intelligence to play dominos!

Back to the kennel with all these tiresome parasites! Back to their silken, padded kennels!

I sing the dirtied dog, the poor dog, the homeless dog, the loafing dog, the acrobat dog, the dog whose instinct, like that of the poor, the gypsy, and the actor, is marvelously sharpened by necessity, that good mother, that true patroness of intellects!

I sing the unlucky dogs, whether those who wander, solitary, in the winding ditches of immense cities, or those who with their blinking, spiritual eyes have said to abandoned men: "Take me with you, and perhaps out of our two miseries we can create a kind of happiness!"

"*Where do the dogs go?*" said Nestor Roqueplan once in an immortal article that he himself has probably forgotten, and which I alone, and maybe Sainte-Beuve, remember still today.[4]

Where do the dogs go, you ask, you inattentive men? They go about their business.

Business meetings, amorous meetings. Through the fog, through the snow, through the mud, in the burning dog-day sun, in the rustling rain they go, they come, they trot, they pass under coaches, impelled by fleas or by passion, by need or by duty. Like us, they get up early in the morning and are trying to make a living or chasing after their pleasures.

Some sleep under some rundown building in the suburbs and come every day at the same hour to beg for scraps at the kitchen door of the Palais-Royal; others run together in packs for more than five leagues to share the charitable meal prepared for them by certain sixty-year-old unwed women, who give their unclaimed hearts to animals because imbecilic men no longer want them.

Others, like runaway slaves mad with love, leave their own territory on certain days to come into the city and frisk for an hour

---

4. Nestor Roqueplan (1804–1870), a theater director and critic; Charles Augustin Sainte-Beuve, the preeminent man of letters in Baudelaire's day. Scholars have been unable to trace the article mentioned here.

around a beautiful bitch who, though she may have neglected her appearance a bit, is proud and grateful.

And they all are very precise and punctual, without needing diaries, notebooks, or pocketbooks.

Have you been to indolent Belgium, and have you admired, as I have, those vigorous dogs hitched to the butcher's cart, or the milkmaid's cart, or the baker's cart, whose triumphant barking testifies to the pleasure and the pride they feel in rivaling horses?

Imagine if you will two dogs who belong to an even more civilized order! Permit me to show you into the room of an absent street performer. A painted wooden bed, no curtains, rumpled bedclothes stained with bedbugs, two straw-backed chairs, an iron stove, one or two broken musical instruments. Oh, the sad furniture! But just look, will you, at those two intelligent characters, dressed in outfits that are somehow both threadbare and luxuriant, as well groomed as troubadours or soldiers, keeping watch like magicians over the *mysterious concoction* simmering on the stove, from which a long spoon protrudes, planted there like one of those high poles perched atop a building to signal that the masonry work is finished.

It is only fair, is it not, that such zealous actors should not be on their way without first filling up their stomachs with some strong, solid soup? And would you begrudge these poor devils their bit of pleasure, since they must confront every day the indifference of the public and the unfairness of the manager who takes the fattest share, and who eats more soup by himself than four actors would?

I have often observed, both smiling at them and touched by them, those four-footed philosophers, those obliging, submissive, devoted slaves whom the republican dictionary could classify as *unofficial* slaves, if the republic, overly concerned with the *happiness* of men, had the time to consider the *honor due to dogs*.

And I have often thought that there might be some place (after all, who knows?) for rewarding so much courage, so much patience and labor, a special paradise for the good dogs, the poor dogs, the stinking and aggrieved dogs. After all, Swedenborg affirms that there is indeed such a special place for the Turks, and another for the Dutch!

The shepherds of Virgil and Theocritus hoped to win, as prizes in their singing contests, a good cheese, a flute made by the best craftsman, or a goat with swollen udders. The poet who sang the poor dogs has received as his prize a fine waistcoat of a color both rich and faded, reminiscent of autumnal suns, of the beauty of matured women, and of Indian summer.

None of those who were present in the tavern on the Rue Villa-Hermosa will ever forget how eagerly the painter stripped off his waistcoat and gave it to the poet,[5] so well did he understand how good and honest a thing it is to sing the poor dogs.

So it was in the old days when a magnificent Italian tyrant would offer the divine Aretino[6] a dagger encrusted with precious stones or a courtly robe in exchange for a precious sonnet or a curious satirical poem.

And every time the poet puts on the painter's waistcoat, he cannot help but think of the good dogs, of the philosopher dogs, of Indian summers, and of the beauty of women no longer young.

---

5. The tavern, in Brussels, was a British one: Horton's Prince of Wales. The painter, Joseph Stevens (see note 1, p. 101), had in fact given Baudelaire such a waistcoat.

6. Pietro Aretino (1492–1556), a satiric poet much admired by Baudelaire.

La Fanfarlo

Samuel Cramer, who in earlier days signed a few romantic follies with the pseudonym of Manuela de Monteverde—back in the good old days of Romanticism—is the contradictory product of a pale German father and a dark Chilean mother. Add to this double origin a French education and literary background, and you will be surprised—or, perhaps, satisfied and edified—by the bizarre complexities of his character. Samuel has a pure, noble brow, eyes that glitter like drops of black coffee, an insolent and sneering nose, impudent and sensual lips, a square, despotic chin, and a pretentiously Raphaelesque head of hair.—He is at once a great idler, pathetically ambitious, and famously unlucky; because he has scarcely had, throughout his whole life, anything beyond half-baked ideas. The sun of laziness that shines at all times around him had dissipated him, and had eaten away that little morsel of genius with which heaven had endowed him. Among all the half-great men I have met in this terrible Parisian life, Samuel was more than any of them the man of bungled masterpieces—an unearthly, fantastic creature whose poetry glittered more in his person than in his works, one who, around one in the morning, between the glare of a coal fire and the ticking of a clock, always seemed to me something like the god of impotence—a modern, hermaphroditic god—an impotence so colossal, so enormous that it seemed epic!

How can I make you understand, make you see clearly this shadowy personality, checkered with sudden flashes of light—at once both slacker and entrepreneur—fecund in difficult schemes and ridiculous aborted ones; a person in whom paradox often took on the proportions of naiveté, and in whom the imagination was as vast as his solitude and absolute idleness? One of Samuel's most natural oddities was to consider himself the equal of those he had come to admire; following his impassioned reading of a beautiful book, his involuntary conclusion was, "Now, this is beautiful enough to have been written by me!" And from there to the conclusion, "therefore, it *is* by me!"—was only about the distance of a hyphen.

In the modern world, this type of character is more common than one would think; the streets, the public walks, the tenements, and all the havens of idlers swarm with creatures like this. And they all identify so completely with this new model that they almost believe they have invented it. Look at them all today, laboriously deciphering the mystical pages of Plotinus or Porphyry;[1] tomorrow, they will all wonder at the fickle and French side of their character, so well depicted by Crébillon the younger.[2] Yesterday, they were in intimate communion with Jerome Cardano;[3] and now look at them laughing with Sterne, or reveling with Rabelais in all the gluttonies of hyperbole. And through it all, they are so pleased with each of their metamorphoses that they don't mind at all being surpassed in posterity's estimation by all those great geniuses.—A naïve and honorable impudence! And such was poor Samuel.

A thoroughly respectable man by birth, and something of a scoundrel by pastime—an actor by temperament—he played out privately for himself incomparable tragedies or, rather, tragicomedies. If gaiety brushed by and tickled him, it had to be acted out, and our gentleman worked hard to laugh heartily. If some memory caused a tear to well up in his eye, he went to the mirror to observe himself weeping. If some girl in an outburst of brutal and juvenile jealousy scratched him with a needle or a penknife, Samuel took his own knife and glorified it into a grander wound, or when he found himself owing some pathetic twenty thousand francs, he cried out joyously, "What a sad, lamentable fate it is to be a genius harassed by debts in the millions!"

But for all that, don't think that he was incapable of true feelings, and that passion only fluttered lightly across his skin. He would have given the shirt off his back for a man he scarcely knew, a man who, on the basis of his face and his handshake, he had just yesterday decided was his closest friend. In matters of the mind and soul, he

---

1. Plotinus (204–270 CE) and Porphyry (c. 233–305 CE) were both Neo-Platonist philosophers with a strong mystical bent.

2. Claude-Prosper de Crébillon (1707–1777) was a novelist whose loose morality and satirical touch contrasts vividly with Plotinus and Porphyry.

3. Girolamo Cardano (1501–1576) was an Italian polymath who wrote on subjects ranging from medicine to mathematics to astrology; he faced heresy charges when he cast the horoscope of Jesus Christ.

showed the lazy contemplation of Germanic natures; in those of passion, his mother's rapid and fickle ardor; and in the practice of life, all the habits of French vanity. He would have got himself wounded in a duel over an author or an artist who had been dead for two centuries. And as he had once been an ardent believer, he later turned passionate atheist. He was at once all the artists he had studied and all the books he had read, and yet, despite this thespian faculty, he remained profoundly original. He was always the gentle, the fantastic, the lazy, the terrible, the sage, the ignorant, the disheveled, the flirtatious Samuel Cramer, the romantic Manuela de Monteverde. He was as infatuated with a friend as with a woman, and loved a woman like a comrade. He possessed the logic of all the fine feelings as well as the science of all the low tricks, and yet he never succeeded in any of them because he believed too much in the impossible. Is it any wonder?—For he was always in the process of imagining the impossible.

Samuel, one evening, took a notion to go out; the air was fine and scented. In keeping with his natural taste for the excessive, his routines of seclusion and dissipation were equally violent and pro-longed, and for a long time now he had faithfully remained in his lodgings. That maternal idleness, that Creole laziness that coursed through his veins kept him from being disturbed by the disorder of his room, of his linen and of his overly dirty and tangled hair. He washed and combed himself, showing how in a matter of moments he was able to reinhabit the clothes and the aplomb of those for whom elegance is an everyday affair; then he opened his window. A warm, golden day burst into the dusty room. Samuel was struck by the way spring had come so suddenly and without any warning in just a few days. He breathed in a warm mild air, pregnant with sweet scents—one part of which ascended to his head, filling it with reverie and desire, while the other part drifted freely downward to his heart, stomach, and liver. With resolve, he snuffed out his two candles, one of which still quivered over a volume of Swedenborg,[4] while the other flickered over one of those shameful books whose

---

4. Emanuel Swedenborg (1688–1772), a Swiss mystical philosopher, interested not only Samuel Cramer but Baudelaire as well, influencing some of his later works.

reading is never profitable except to those possessed of an immoderate taste for the truth.

From the height of his solitude, encumbered by useless papers, piled with old books and peopled with his daydreams, Samuel had often observed a certain form and figure strolling down one of the pathways of the Luxembourg Gardens, a form similar to one he had once loved in the country—at the age when one is in love with love. Her figure, though somewhat more mature and thickened by several years of use, had the thorough, decent grace of a respectable woman; in the depths of her eyes you could still sometimes glimpse the teary reveries of the young girl. She came and went, always escorted by an elegant enough maid, whose look and style, though, suggested she was more a companion than a domestic. She seemed to seek out isolated areas, and she would seat herself in the sad posture of a widow, sometimes holding in her distracted hand a book that she never read.

Samuel had known her in the neighborhood of Lyons,[5] young, alert, playful, and thinner. By observing her closely and in order to, so to speak, recognize her, he tried to recapture one by one all the slivers of memory connected to her in his imagination; he narrated to himself, detail by detail, the whole youthful novel, which had since become lost amid the preoccupations of his life and the labyrinth of his passions.

That evening, he bowed to her, but very carefully and discreetly. As he passed by, he heard this scrap of dialogue behind him:

"What do you think of that young man, Mariette?" But this was said in so absent-minded a tone of voice that even the most malicious observer could find nothing in it with which to reproach the lady.

"I like him very well, Madame. Madame knows that it's Samuel Cramer?"

And in a more severe voice: "And how would you know that, Mariette?"

This is why, the next day, Samuel took great care to retrieve for her the book and handkerchief he found on a bench, which

---

5. Baudelaire, like his character Cramer, spent four years of his adolescence near Lyons (1832–1836).

however she had not lost, for she was standing nearby watching the sparrows battle over some crumbs, or seeming to contemplate the inner workings of the shrubbery. While it often happens that conversation can begin abruptly between two souls that fate has elevated to the same level, he nonetheless felt a bizarre happiness to find in her someone disposed both to listen and respond to him.

"Have I the good fortune, Madame, to remain in some corner of your memory? Or am I so changed that you cannot recognize in me the childhood companion with whom you once deigned to play both hide-and-seek and hooky?"

"A woman," she replied with a half-smile, "does not enjoy the right to recall people so readily; and so I must thank you, Monsieur, for taking the initiative and recalling to me those lovely and happy memories. And then . . . every year of living contains so many events, so many thoughts . . . and it does seem to me that there have been many years?"

"Many years," Samuel said, "which for me have been sometimes slow, sometimes quick to fly away, but all cruel in their own ways!"

"But their poetry?" asked the lady with a smile in her eyes.

"Always, Madame!" Samuel replied, laughing. "But what are you reading?"

"A Walter Scott novel."[6]

"Now I understand your frequent interruptions! Oh, that tedious author! A dusty exhumer of chronicles! A fastidious mass of descriptions of bric-a-brac, a heap of old and castoff things of every sort—armor, tableware, furniture, gothic inns, and melodramatic castles, where lifeless mannequins stalk about, dressed in leotards and gaudy doublets—tired stereotypes that no plagiarist of eighteen would dream of touching again ten years later; impossible esquires, and lovers entirely devoid of reality—no truths of the heart, no philosophy of feeling! How different with our good French novelists, in whom passion and morality are carried over even to the description of physical objects! Who cares if the chatelaine wears a ruff or crinolines by Oudinot,[7] so long as her sobs and treasons are believable? Is

---

6. Scott's historical novels, wildly popular among the generation preceding Baudelaire's, were often scoffed at by the young avant-garde of Baudelaire's generation.

7. Achille Oudinot's designs, especially his crinolines, were highly popular in the era.

a lover more interesting if he carries a dagger in his waistcoat instead of a visiting card, and does a tyrant dressed in a black coat cause a less poetical fear than does one garbed in leather and iron?"

Samuel, as you see, belonged to that class of man called "serious" —impassioned and intolerable, men whose vocation ruins their conversation; men for whom every occasion, every acquaintance, even one struck up on the street or beneath a tree, even with a ragman, is a fine occasion for the opinionated expression of their ideas. The only difference between traveling salesmen, wandering industrialists, stock exchange know-it-alls, and "serious" poets is the difference between advertising and preaching; the vice of these latter is entirely disinterested.

The lady replied simply, "Monsieur Samuel, I am only a common reader, which is to say an innocent one. So I can find pleasure easily in anything. But let's speak about you: I would be very happy if you would consider me worthy of reading some of your works."

"But, Madame, how can it be . . . ?" replied the surprised poet's enormous vanity.

"The man who runs my reading room says he's never heard of you." And she smiled sweetly to minimize the effect of the teasing comment.

"Madame," Samuel said sententiously, "the true public in the nineteenth century is made up of women; your approval will make me greater than twenty academies could."

"Well then, Monsieur, I will hold you to your promise.— Mariette, my parasol and scarf; *they* may be waiting for us at home. You know that Monsieur comes home early."

She made a brief, graceful bow, with nothing compromising about it, and with a familiarity that was still dignified.

Samuel was not surprised to find an old flame now subject to a conjugal bond. In the universal history of sentiment, this sort of thing was in fact required. She was called Madame de Cosmelly, and she lived in one of the most aristocratic streets of the Faubourg Saint-Germain.

The next day he found her, her head tilted toward the flowerbeds in a graceful and almost studied melancholy, and offered her his volume of *Ospreys*, a collection of sonnets like the ones we've all written and all read, back in the days when our ideas were short and our hair was long.

Samuel was very curious to learn whether these *Ospreys* had stirred the soul of the beautiful melancholic, and whether the cries of these wicked birds had spoken in his favor; but a few days later she told him, with a brutal candor and honesty:

"Monsieur, I am only a woman, and consequently my judgment counts for little; but it seems to me that the sorrows and the loves of authors do not much resemble the sorrows and loves of other people. You write very elegant gallantries, no doubt, of the sort that women will find exquisite, exquisite enough that they perhaps should be feared. You sing the beauty of mothers in a style that must lose you the approval of their daughters. You tell us that you are head over heels in love with Madame so-and-so who, let us suppose for the sake of her honor, spends less time reading you than mending socks and mittens for her children. But then, by the most extraordinary contrast, and by some mysterious cause I cannot fathom, you reserve your most mystical incense for bizarre creatures who read even less than those ladies, and you swoon platonically for those underworld sultanesses who ought, I would think, when confronted with the sensitive gaze of a poet, to open their eyes wider than the eyes of cattle who awake to find themselves in the middle of a forest fire. And then I can't see why you cherish funereal subject matters and anatomical descriptions. When one is young and when one has, as you do, a real talent and all the conditions necessary for happiness, it would seem to me more natural to celebrate health and the joys of a decent gentleman rather than to exercise your wits on anathemas, and to converse with *Ospreys*."

And how did he respond to this? "Madame, pity me, or rather pity us, because I have many brothers of my type; it's the hatred of everything and of ourselves that leads us toward these lies. It's because we despair of becoming noble and beautiful by natural means that we put such bizarre makeup on our faces. We have so assiduously applied ourselves to cultivating our hearts, we have put them so intently under the microscope to study their hideous growths and warts, which we have encouraged to grow and expand, that it has become impossible for us to speak as other men do. They live in order to live, and we, alas, we live in order to know. There is the entire mystery. Age alters only the voice, and ruins only the hair and the teeth; we have altered the natural accent, we have eradicated, one by one, the innocent reticences that bristle in the interior of the respectable man. We have psychologized like those madmen who only worsen their madness by trying to understand it. The years weaken only the physical body, but we have deformed the feelings. Cursed, three times cursed be those sickly fathers who made us into weaklings ridden with rickets, predestined as we are to engender nothing but stillbirths!"

"The *Ospreys* again!" she said. "Come, give me your arm, and let us admire these poor flowers that the spring has made so happy!"

Instead of admiring the flowers, Samuel Cramer, in whom both phrases and sentences had started to sprout, proceeded to take a few bad stanzas he had composed in his finest manner, rearrange them into prose, and begin declaiming. The lady let him go on.

"What a difference there is—and how little of the same person remains, apart from the memory! But memory itself only brings new pain. Those beautiful days, when morning did not bring with it those pains in our knees, sluggish or stiff from dreaming, when our clear eyes smiled upon all nature, when we did not reason but simply lived and enjoyed; when our sighs escaped gently, silently, and without pride! How many times have I seen again, in my imagination, one of those lovely autumnal evenings where young hearts make the same sudden progress that young trees do, shooting up all at once after the lightning bolt of love. Then I see, I sense, I listen; the moon awakens huge butterflies; the warm wind opens the night flowers; the water in the fountains lies sleeping. Listen, in your heart, to the quick, sudden waltz from that mysterious piano. The scents from the storm enter in by the windows; it is the hour when the garden is clothed in red and white dresses, unafraid of the damp. The obliging bushes hook on the flouncing skirts; brown hair and blonde curls mingle in a kind of whirlwind!—Do you still remember, Madame, those enormous haystacks, so easily slid down, the old nurse so slow in her pursuit, and the clock so prompt to bring you back under the eyes of your aunt, in the great dining room?"

Madame de Cosmelly interrupted Samuel with a sigh, and was about to open her mouth, no doubt to beg him to stop, but he had already started up again.

"The saddest thing," he said, "is that every love has an unhappy ending, and all the more unhappy in proportion to how divinely it began, with what wings it first took flight. There is no dream, no matter how ideal, that does not end with a greedy brat hanging from its breast; there is no hideaway, no cabin so delicious and obscure, that the pickaxe will not find and attack. Now all this is only material destruction; but there is another kind, more pitiless and more secret, that attacks invisible things. Consider that, at the very moment when you lean closely upon the being you have chosen, and when you say to him, 'let us fly away together, and seek out the depths of the sky'—an implacable, serious voice bends to your ear to tell you that our passions are liars, that beautiful faces are the creations of our myopia, and beautiful souls the creations of our ignorance, and that a day will inevitably come when the idol, now seen clearly, is merely an object, not just of hatred, but of contempt and shock!"

"No more, Monsieur," said Madame de Cosmelly.

She was obviously moved; Samuel could see that his knife had pierced an old wound, and he went on, with cruelty.

"Madame," he said, "the bracing miseries of memory have their charms, and in the intoxication of sorrow one sometimes finds consolation.—At this somber warning, all those loyal souls will cry out: 'Lord, lift me up from this place with my dream intact and pure; I want to give my passion to the world in all its innocence, and to keep my wreath unwithered.' But the results of disillusionment are terrible. The sickly children born from a dying love are debauchery and hideous impotence: debauchery of the spirit, and impotence of the heart, making the one live on only out of curiosity, and the other die every day of boredom. We are all more or less like a traveler who has traversed a very large country; he watches the sun, which once gilded superbly all the charms of his route, now sink down upon a flat horizon. He seats himself, resignedly, on a dirty hill covered with unknown debris, and he says to the scents arising from the briars that they mount to the empty sky in vain; to the few, miserable seeds, that they germinate in vain in this dried-out soil; to the birds who feel their marriages have been blessed by someone, that they are wrong to build their nests in a country so beaten by cold, violent winds. He sadly resumes his path toward a desert that he knows is similar to the one he just crossed, escorted by the pale phantom they call Reason, who lights up the aridity of his path with a weak lantern, and who, when the thirst of passion comes back from time to time, quenches it with the poison of ennui."

Suddenly he heard a deep sigh and a barely concealed sob, and he turned to face Madame de Cosmelly; she was weeping copiously, and she no longer had the strength to hide her tears.

He watched her for a time in silence, putting on his tenderest, most unctuous air; the brutal, hypocritical actor was proud of those beautiful tears, seeing them as his own work, his literary property. He misunderstood the real meaning of this sorrow, just as Madame de Cosmelly misunderstood the look he was giving her. There followed a singular game of miscomprehensions for a moment, after which Samuel Cramer took her hand in both of his, which she accepted trustingly.

"Madame," Samuel began after a few moments of silence—that classical silence that denotes great emotion—"true wisdom consists less in cursing than in hope. Without that divine gift of hope, how could we traverse the hideous desert of ennui that I've just described? The phantom that accompanies us is truly a phantom of reason; he can be chased away by sprinkling him with the holy water of hope, the first theological virtue. There is an amiable philosophy that can find consolation in what would seem to be the most unworthy objects. Just as virtue is worth more than innocence, and as there is more merit in sowing seed in a desert than in gathering fruits in a healthy orchard, just so is it good for a higher soul to purify itself and to purify its neighbor with its contact. And just as there is really no unpardonable betrayal, so there is no fault of which one cannot be absolved, no lapse of memory that cannot be overcome; it is the science of loving one's neighbor and finding him loveable, and the art of living well. The more delicate a spirit is, the more it discovers original beauties; the more tender a soul is, and the more open to divine hope, the more it finds in others, no matter how soiled, motives for love; this is the work of charity, and one has seen more than one voyager, sorrowing and lost in the arid deserts of disillusionment, reconquer her faith and her love for what she had lost, more powerfully now that she has mastered the technique of directing her passion and that of her beloved."

Madame de Cosmelly's face had slowly cleared; her sorrow now shone with hope like a watery sun, and Samuel had barely finished his speech when she spoke with the eager and naïve ardor of a child.

"Is it really true, Monsieur, that it's possible, that there really are branches so easily grasped by the desperate?"

"Certainly, Madame."

"Oh, you would make me the happiest of women if you would see fit to give me your recipe!"

"Nothing easier," he replied brutally.

In the process of this sentimental banter, trust had arisen, and had in effect united the hands of the two, so much so that after a few hesitations and a few pruderies that Samuel thought augured well, Madame de Cosmelly in turn began her confidences thus:

"I understand, Monsieur, all that a poetic soul must suffer in that isolation, and how an ambitious heart like yours must eat itself up in its solitude; but your sorrows, which belong only to you, originate, as far as I can decipher them beneath the pomp of your language, in bizarre, unsatisfied, and almost unsatisfiable needs. You suffer, true; but perhaps it's your suffering that creates your grandeur, and it is as necessary to you as happiness is to others. —Now, please deign to listen, and sympathize with troubles that are easier to understand—a provincial sorrow? I ask for counsel from you, Monsieur Cramer, from you, the savant, the man of intelligence—counsel and perhaps help for a friend.

"You know that in the days when you knew me I was a good girl, a little dreamy like you, but timid and entirely obedient; I observed myself in the mirror less often than you, and I always hesitated to eat or put in my pocket the peaches and grapes you had bravely stolen for me from our neighbors' vines. I never found a pleasure to be truly agreeable and complete unless it had been permitted, and I much preferred embracing a fine young man like you in front of my old aunt rather than out in the meadows. The coquetry and the pains taken over appearance that are necessary for every marriage-able girl came late for me. When I learned how to sing a little at the piano, I was dressed with intense care, and taught to keep my back rigid; I was made to do gymnastics, and I was forbidden to spoil my hands by planting flowers or raising pet birds. I wasn't permitted to read much beyond Berquin,[8] and I was dressed up elaborately and taken to see bad operas. When Monsieur de Cosmelly came to the chateau, I was seized right away by a powerful feeling of friendship for him; comparing his flourishing youth to my aging, rather grouchy aunt, I found in him very noble and decent qualities, and he treated me with the most respectful gallantry. And then people mentioned some even more attractive traits: an arm broken in a duel defending the sister of a cowardly friend; enormous sums loaned to impoverished old friends; and who knows what else. He had, around everyone, a commanding air that was both affable and irresistible, an air that mastered me altogether. How had he lived before he came to stay at the chateau? Had he known other pleasures besides hunting with me or singing virtuous lyrics to accompany my wretched piano-playing; had he had mistresses? I knew nothing about it, and I never ever dreamed of trying to learn. I set myself to love him, with all the credulity of a girl who never had the chance to do any com-paring, and I married him—which gave my aunt the greatest pleas-ure. When I became his wife in the eyes of religion and of the law, I loved him even more.—I loved him too much, that's certain.—Was I wrong, was I right? Who can say? I was happy in this love, and I was wrong not to know that there might be problems.—Did I know him well before marrying him? No, not at all; but it seems to me that one can no more accuse a decent girl who wants to marry of making an imprudent choice, than a ruined woman of taking an unworthy lover. The one and the other—miserable as we are!—are equally ignorant. These unlucky victims that we call marriage-able girls lack an education in shame, that is, an understanding of a man's vices. I wish that all of those poor girls, before they submit to the conjugal bond, could secretly listen to two men conversing

---

8. Arnaud Berquin (1749–1791) was the author of widely popular children's stories, such as *L'Ami des enfants* (1782); his books were popular in part because they were entirely inoffensive.

about life, and especially about women. After this first, fearful test, they could less dangerously deliver themselves up to the terrible hazards of marriage, aware now of both the strengths and weaknesses of their future tyrants."

Samuel couldn't tell exactly where this charming victim was heading; but he was beginning to think that she was talking too much about her husband to be a truly disillusioned woman.

After a few minutes' pause, as if she feared to broach the darkest topic, she began again: "One day, Monsieur de Cosmelly wanted to return to Paris; I deserved the chance to shine, and I should be seen in a frame worthy of me. A beautiful, educated woman, he said, belongs in Paris. She should know how to display herself in society, and let some of her radiance fall upon her husband.—A woman with a noble spirit and good sense knows that the only glory she can expect in this life is to make herself a part of the glory of her traveling companion, to serve her husband's virtues, and above all, she will only be respected to the degree that she makes him respected. —Of course, this was the simplest and surest way for him to get me to obey him almost with joy; to know that my efforts and my obedience enhanced me in his eyes, nothing more was needed to make me decide to come to grips with this terrible Paris—of which I was instinctively afraid—as if there was a dark, dazzling phantom on the horizon of my dreams that made my poor little loving heart shrink. —And there, clearly, was the true motive for our trip. A husband's vanity creates the virtue of a woman in love. Perhaps he lied to himself, in a kind of good faith, and tricked his own conscience without quite realizing it.—In Paris, we had days reserved for close friends, with whom Monsieur de Cosmelly eventually grew bored, just as he grew bored with his wife. Perhaps he even developed a distaste for her, because she loved him too much; she wore her heart on her sleeve. He took a dislike to his friends for the opposite reason; they had nothing to offer him except the monotonous pleasures of conversations in which passion played no part. Soon, his activities took a different direction. After the friends came horses and gambling. The hum and buzz of society, and the sight of people who had managed to avoid entanglements, and who told him endless stories of their wild and busy youth, pulled him away from the fireside and lengthy conversations. He, the man who never had any affairs beyond those of his heart, now became a man of business. Wealthy and without any profession, he now managed to create a whole crowd of bustling frivolities that filled up all his time. Those marital questions—"Where are you going?"—"When will you be back?"—"Come back soon"—I had to choke all those back, because now the English life—that death of the heart—the life of clubs and circles absorbed him entirely. The pains he took with his appearance and the dandyism he affected shocked me at first; it was obvious that I was not its object. I wanted to do the same, to be more than beautiful, to become a coquette, a coquette for him, as he was for everyone else; in the past, I offered everything, I gave everything, and now I wanted to make him beg for it. I wanted to stir up the ashes of my dead happiness, to try to make them return to life; but apparently I am no good with ruses and entirely maladroit at vice, because he never even seemed to notice my efforts.—My aunt, as cruel as all old envious women reduced to being spectators when they once were actresses, and forced to contemplate the joys that are no longer available to them, took great care to inform me, via an intermediary cousin, that my husband was quite taken with a fashionable woman of the theater. I got myself taken to all the shows, and with every slightly beautiful woman who came on the stage, I shuddered to see my rival in her. Finally, I learned, through the charity of that same cousin, that it was La Fanfarlo,[9] a dancer as beautiful as she was stupid.—As a writer, you must certainly have met her.—I am not overly vain nor overly proud of my looks; but I swear to you, Monsieur Cramer, that many nights at three or four in the morning, worn out with waiting for my husband, my eyes red with crying and insomnia, after having said many prayers begging for my husband to return to fidelity and duty, I've asked God, and my conscience, and my mirror, if I were as beautiful as this wretched Fanfarlo. My mirror and my conscience have replied, "Yes." God has forbidden me to glorify myself, but not to enjoy a legitimate victory. So why, then, between two equal beauties, do men so often prefer the flower that

---

9. The stage name of Fanfarlo is evidently Baudelaire's invention, but there were dancers with similar names, notably one named Fanfarnou. Pichois (OC I, 1422) notes that the name might suggest "fanfare."

everybody has sniffed to the one that has remained faithfully hidden away in the most secret, private pathways of the marital garden? And why is it that these women who are so prodigal with their bodies—that treasure whose key should be held by one sultan only—attract more adorers than we do, we unhappy victims of a single love? What is the magic charm with which vice creates an aureole around these creatures? And what is the awkward repulsiveness that virtue gives to certain others? Explain it to me, you who by profession must know all life's inclinations and their various causes!"

Samuel had no time to reply, for she continued with ardor:

"Monsieur de Cosmelly has some serious things on his conscience, that is if God cares about the fall of a young and virginal soul that he created to give happiness to someone. If Monsieur de Cosmelly were to die this very night, he would have to implore God's mercy many times over; because he has, through his own fault, taught his wife many ugly feelings—hatred, mistrust of her beloved, and the thirst for vengeance.—Ah, Monsieur! I pass sorrowful nights in restless insomnia; I pray, I curse, I blaspheme. The priest tells me we must carry our cross with resignation; but there can be no resignation when love has turned to madness, and faith has been shaken. My confessor is not a woman, and I love my husband, I love him, Monsieur, with all the passion and all the misery of a mistress trampled under foot. There is nothing that I haven't tried. Instead of the simple and somber clothes he used to look upon with pleasure, I've put on the insane and sumptuous outfits of a woman of the theater. And I, the chaste spouse that he had to go to the depths of an impoverished chateau to find, I have paraded before him in the dresses of a slut; I've made myself clever and sprightly when I've felt death at my heart. I have embellished my despair with glittering smiles. And alas, he never even noticed. Monsieur, I've even put on rouge!—Well, as you see, it's a banal story, the same story as all the miserable ones—a novel of the provinces!"

While she sobbed, Samuel was like Tartuffe in the grasp of Orgon,[10] the unexpected husband who bursts from the depths of his

---

10. Tartuffe is the religious hypocrite in Molière's play (1664) of the same name; Orgon is the credulous husband who ultimately discovers Tartuffe's true character.

hiding place, like the virtuous sobs of this lady bursting from her heart and seizing the staggering hypocrisy of the poet by the collar.

Madame de Cosmelly's extreme abandon, her freedom and her trust had emboldened him prodigiously but had not surprised him. Samuel Cramer, who had so often shocked others, was rarely shocked himself. He seemed to want to put into practice and to demonstrate the truth of Diderot's aphorism: "Incredulity is often the vice of the fool, and credulity that of the men of intelligence. The intelligent man sees deeply into the immensity of possibility. The fool scarcely thinks what is right in front of him is possible. This is perhaps what renders the one a coward and the other foolhardy."[11] This explains everything. Some scrupulous readers, those who love for truth to be believable, will no doubt find much to criticize in this story, whereas in fact my only labor has been to change the names and accentuate some details; how is it, they will say, that Samuel, a poet of low style and worse morals, could engage so adeptly with a woman like Madame de Cosmelly? To shower her, apropos of a Scott novel, with such a torrent of romantic and banal poetry? And Madame de Cosmelly, this decent and virtuous spouse, how could she turn and shower him, without modesty and without suspicion, with the secrets of her sorrows? To which I reply that Madame de Cosmelly had the simplicity of a beautiful soul, and that Samuel was as bold as butterflies, May bugs, and poets; he hurled himself into every flame, and came in through every window. Diderot's aphorism explains why the one was so open, the other so brusque and so impudent. It also explains all the blunders that Samuel had committed in his life, blunders that a fool would not have committed. That part of the public who are essentially cowards will hardly be able to understand a character like Samuel, who was essentially credulous and imaginative, to the point where he believed—as a poet, in his public—and as a man, in his own passions.

Before long, he perceived that this woman was stronger, deeper than her air suggested, and that it wouldn't do to attack this candid piety head on. He paraded anew his romantic jargon to her. Ashamed of having been stupid, he now determined to be decadent;

---

11. Denis Diderot, *Pensées Philosophiques* (1746), xxxii.

he spoke for a while in his seminarian's patois of closing wounds, or of cauterizing them by opening new ones, larger ones, without pain. Anyone lacking the absolute force of a Valmont or a Lovelace[12] who wants to seduce an honest woman who suspects nothing is quite familiar with the comic and emphatic clumsiness with which everyone offers his heart saying, "Please, accept this absurdity." This will obviate, then, any need for me to explain how stupid Samuel was. Madame de Cosmelly, that loveable Elmira[13] with the clear and prudent eyesight of virtue, saw at once the role she could have this novice scoundrel play in serving both her honor and her husband's. She repaid him in the same coin; she let him press her hands; they spoke of friendship and things Platonic. She murmured the word "vengeance"; she said that, in the miserable crises that occur in women's lives, many would willingly give the remainder of their heart to the avenger, that part of the heart that the villain had left them—along with other absurdities and stage-play phrases. In short, she played the coquette out of a moral motive, and our young decadent, who was more simpleton than sage, promised to snatch La Fanfarlo from Monsieur de Cosmelly and rid him of this courtesan—hoping to find in the arms of the honest woman the recompense that this feat merited.—Only poets are simple enough to invent this sort of monstrosity.

A sufficiently comic detail of this story, which was something of an interlude in the sad drama playing out among the four characters, was the mistake involving Samuel's sonnets; for, in the matter of sonnets, he was incorrigible: one was for Madame de Cosmelly, where he praised in mystical style her Beatrice-like[14] beauty, her voice, the angelic purity of her eyes, the chastity of her conduct, etc., and the other was for La Fanfarlo, to whom he served up a ragout of spiced-up gallantries calculated to move the blood of the most jaded palate, a poetic genre in which he excelled, and in which he had

---

12. Valmont and Lovelace are the seducer heroes of, respectively, Pierre Choderlos de Laclos' *Les liaisons dangereuses* (1782) and Samuel Richardson's *Clarissa* (1747–1748).

13. Elmira is the virtuous wife in *Tartuffe*. The repeated allusions to the play emphasize Baudelaire's theme of hypocrisy.

14. Beatrice is the saintly muse and beloved of Dante in *The Divine Comedy*.

early on surpassed all the Andalusian[15] exoticisms possible. Now, the former tidbit arrived at the dancer's, who tossed this collection of nonsense in the cigar box; the second went to the poor forsaken one who at first read it with widening eyes, then understood what had happened, and despite all her sorrows could not help but laugh heartily, as in better days.

Samuel went to the theater to study La Fanfarlo on the boards. He found her light-footed, magnificent, vigorous, absolutely tasteful in her costumes, and decided that Monsieur de Cosmelly was very lucky in being able to ruin himself for such a piece.

He went to her home twice—a cottage with velvet-covered stair steps, stuffed with curtains and carpets, in a new and leafy quarter of town; but he could find no reasonable pretext for introducing himself. A declaration of love could be futile and even dangerous. If he failed, he would be unable to come back. And apart from that, he learned that she never received visitors. A few close friends saw her from time to time. What would he say or do in the home of a dancer so magnificently set up and kept, and so idolized by her lover? What could he bring to her, he who was neither tailor, nor dressmaker, nor ballet-master, nor millionaire?—He therefore settled on a simple and crude scheme: La Fanfarlo must come to him. In that era, critical articles of praise or condemnation had much more power than they do today. The "abilities" of the newspaper, as a grand lawyer recently put it in the course of a sadly notorious trial,[16] were then much greater than they are now; a few talented people having once surrendered to the journalists, their giddy and adventuresome insolence no longer knew any bounds. Samuel thus undertook—a man who knew not one word about music—to specialize in lyric theater.

---

15. The term "Andalusian" here suggests the romantic and exotic, and probably signals an allusion to Alfred de Musset's *Tales of Spain and Italy* (1832), a book of poems heavily indebted to Byron.

16. Graham Robb argues convincingly that the passage alludes to the 1846 trial of a journalist named Beauvallon who killed one of his colleagues, named Dujarier, in a duel. Dujarier's mistress—and the catalyst of the quarrel—was the famous and scandalous dancer, Lola Montez. Robb argues that the character of La Fanfarlo is directly modeled on Montez. His argument is summarized in his translation of Claude Pichois' biography, *Baudelaire* (London: Hamish Hamilton, 1989), 133–37.

From then on, La Fanfarlo was chopped to bits on a weekly basis by an important newspaper. Of course, you could not say, or even suggest, that her leg, ankle, or knees were badly formed; the muscles rippled beneath the stockings, and all the lorgnettes would have cried out, blasphemy! So, she was instead accused of being brutal, common, devoid of taste, of wanting to import German and Spanish habits into the ballet; castanets, spurs, heels—not to mention that she drank like a grenadier, that she loved little dogs and the daughter of her servant too much—and other dirty linen from her private life, those areas where certain minor newspapers graze and batten on a daily basis. With the tactic peculiar to journalists, who love to compare utterly disparate items, she was contrasted with an ethereal dancer who always dressed in white, and whose chaste movements never disturbed the audience's conscience. Sometimes, when La Fanfarlo achieved an especially difficult leap, she would cry out and laugh aloud in the direction of the pit; she dared to dance even while walking. She never wore those insipid gauze dresses that let you see everything while divining nothing. She liked material that made some sound, long skirts, crackling, spangled, ornamented with tin jewelry, that had to be raised high by a vigorous knee, and tumbler's blouses. She danced, not with earrings, but with huge pendants that I would call almost chandeliers. She would willingly have had a crowd of those bizarre little dolls attached to the hem of her skirt, like those old gypsy women who tell your fortune with a menacing air, whom you can meet at noon under the arches of Roman ruins; all those comical touches, in short, that the romantic Samuel, one of the last romantics still stalking France, loved passionately.

So much so that after having denigrated La Fanfarlo for three months running, he fell hopelessly in love with her, and she for her part wanted to know who was this monster, this heart of brass, this pedant, this impoverished spirit who so stubbornly denied the royalty of her genius.

We must do this justice to La Fanfarlo, to say that on her part this was only a matter of curiosity, nothing more. Did such a man actually have a nose in the middle of his face, and did he really conform to the rest of the species? When she had obtained some bits of information about Samuel Cramer, when she had learned that he was a man like any other, with some sense and some talent, she understood vaguely that there was something less mysterious about it all, and that these terrible Monday articles might very well be only a sort of weekly bouquet, or the visiting card of a stubborn petitioner.

He met her one night in her dressing room. Two enormous candlesticks and a fire cast a trembling light on the gaudy costumes hanging around the boudoir.

The queen of this realm, as soon as she left the stage, put on the clothing of a simple mortal and now, squatting on a chair, she was shamelessly lacing her boot on her adorable leg. Her hands, stout but tapered, played the laces across the eyelets of her boots with the agility of a shuttle, with no thought of the skirt that ought to have been pulled down. That leg was already, for Samuel, the object of an infinite desire. Long, thin, stout, and sinewy all at once, it had all the exactitude of the beautiful and all the libertine attraction of the pretty. Sliced perpendicularly at its broadest point, the leg would have formed a kind of triangle whose summit was situated at the tibia, and whose softly rounded calf line would have formed the convex base. A real man's leg is too hard, and the woman's legs sketched by Devéria[17] are too soft to give the idea.

In this agreeable pose, her head, bent down toward her foot, exposed the neck of a proconsul, big and strong, allowing one to infer the grooves of her shoulder blades, clothed in their dark and abundant flesh. Her heavy, thick hair tumbled forward on both sides just tickling her breast and obscuring her eyes, so that she constantly had to disturb it by pushing it back. The woman and her clothing were imbued with an insolent and charming impatience, like that of an annoyed child who finds that things are not moving quickly enough, an impatience that continually uncovered new points of view, new effects of line and color.

Samuel paused respectfully—or feigned pausing respectfully, because, with this devil of a man, the great problem is always knowing at what point the actor takes over.

---

17. Achille Devéria (1800–1857), a painter and popular illustrator who also executed many erotic pictures.

"Ah, there you are, Monsieur," she said without stopping what she was doing, though she had been informed of Samuel's visit a few minutes before. "You have something to ask me, I understand?"

The sublime impudence of her phrasing went straight to poor Samuel's heart; he could chatter like a romantic magpie for a week at a time with Madame de Cosmelly; here, he responded quietly: "Yes, Madame." And tears started to his eyes.

This was a great success; La Fanfarlo smiled.

"What insect has stung you, Monsieur, to make you tear me apart so? What a horrible profession . . ."

"Horrible it is, Madame. It's because I adore you."

"I thought so," La Fanfarlo replied. "But you are a monster; these are abominable tactics.—Poor girls that we are!" she added, laughing. "Flora, my bracelet.—Give me your arm, and take me to my coach, and tell me if you think I was good tonight?"

They went out arm in arm, like two old friends; Samuel was in love, or at least he felt his heart beating strongly.—He might be utterly peculiar, but this time he definitely was not ridiculous.

In his joy, he almost forgot to tell Madame de Cosmelly of his success, and to dispatch a little hope to her lonely sitting room.

A few days later, La Fanfarlo danced the role of Columbine in a sprawling pantomime arranged for her by some of her enthusiasts. She went through a pleasant series of metamorphoses, from Columbine to Marguerite to Elvira to Zephyrine,[18] gaily embracing in turn several generations of characters borrowed from diverse countries and diverse literatures. A great musician condescended to provide a fantastical score to match the bizarreness of the subject matter. La Fanfarlo was by turns respectable, elfin, mad, playful; she was sublime in her art, acting with her legs and dancing with her eyes.

In passing, we might note that nowadays the art of the dance is too much scorned. All the great cultures, beginning with the ancient world and including those of India and Arabia, have cultivated it as the equal of poetry. For some pagan groups, dance is as superior to

18. Four famous roles: Columbine is Pierrot's beloved in the many plays of the eighteenth-century Commedia dell'arte; Marguerite is from *Faust;* Elvira is from Mozart's opera *Don Giovanni;* and Zephyrine is from the vaudeville comedy *Les Saltimbanques* (1838) by Charles Varin and Théophile Dumersan.

music as the visible and created world is superior to the invisible and uncreated.—This may be clear only to those who understand that music provides ideas for painting.—Dance can reveal all that is mysterious in music, and it has the additional merit of being human and palpable. Dance is poetry with arms and legs; it is matter—gracious, terrible, animated—embellished by movements.—Terpischore is a muse of the Midi;[19] I presume that she was very dark, and that her feet often beat through golden fields of wheat; her movements, embodying a precise cadence, provide divine motifs for sculpture. But the Catholic La Fanfarlo, not content to be only Terpischore's rival, called to her aid all the art of more modern divinities. The mists intermingled with the forms of fairies and undines less vaporous and less nonchalant. She was at the same time a Shakespearean caprice and an Italian clown.

The poet was ravished; he believed he saw before him the dreams of his very earliest days. He could have capered about her dressing room ridiculously, even cracking his head against something in the mad intoxication that dominated him.

A small and perfectly closed coach rapidly carried the poet and the dancer to the little house I've described.

Our man expressed his admiration by the mute kisses he applied feverishly to her feet and hands.—And she was fascinated too, not just by the power of his charm, but because she had never seen a man so bizarre nor a passion so electrifying.

The night was as black as the tomb, and as the wind rocked the masses of clouds, it shook from them a streaming downpour of hail and rain. A great wind rattled the attics and brought groans from the steeples. The gutter, funeral bed of yesterday's love letters and orgies, carried its thousand secrets frothing toward the sewers; mortality fell rapturously on the hospitals, and the Chattertons and Savages[20] of the Rue Saint-Jacques clenched their freezing fingers on their writing desks—when the most false, most egotistical, most sensual, most

---

19. Terpsichore is the classical muse of dance and song. The Midi is the south of France.

20. Richard Savage (1698–1743) and Thomas Chatterton (1752–1770) had become iconic figures representing the tragically impoverished, misunderstood, persecuted poet.

greedy and cleverest of our friends arrived for a fine supper and gorgeous table, in the company of one of the most beautiful women that nature ever shaped to please the eye. Samuel wanted to open the window to cast his conquering eye on the accursed city; then, lowering his gaze to all the various delights that he had around him, he hastened to his pleasure.

In the company of such things, he must naturally become eloquent; and La Fanfarlo found him almost handsome despite the wild thicket of his hair and his appraiser's nose.

Samuel and La Fanfarlo had exactly the same views on cuisine and on the alimentary system necessary to elite beings. Simple meats and bland fish were excluded from the siren's meals. Champagne rarely dishonored her table. The most celebrated Bordeaux with the finest bouquets bowed to the dense, heavy troop of Burgundies, of wines from Auvergne, Anjou, and the Midi, and of the foreign wines of Germany, Greece, Spain. Samuel was in the habit of saying that a glass of real wine should resemble a cluster of black grapes, and that one should have to eat it as much as drink it.—La Fanfarlo liked her meat bloody and her wines potent. But for all that, she was never drunk.—Both of them professed a sincere and profound admiration for truffles. The truffle, that secret and mysterious vegetation of Cybele,[21] that savory sickness that she hides in her entrails longer than the most precious of metals, that exquisite matter that challenges the agronomist's wisdom, as gold did the alchemist Paracelsus; the truffle, marking the distinction between the ancient and the modern world,[22] which, after a glass of Chio, has the effect of a long set of zeroes following a number.

As for the issue of sauces, dressings, and seasonings, a serious question that would require a whole chapter as serious as a scientific journal, I can assure you that they were perfectly in accord, and above all on the necessity of applying the whole of nature's pharmacy to aid the cuisine. Pimentos, English powders, saffrons, colonial substances, exotic dustings, all of it seemed good to them, not to mention musk and incense. If Cleopatra came back to life, I am

---

21. Cybele was the goddess of the earth.

22. *The truffles of the Romans were white and of a different species than ours.* [Baudelaire's note.]

convinced that she would have wanted to season her beef or venison filets with Arabian perfumes. Certainly, it is deplorable that today's best chefs are not required by a particular and voluptuary law to understand the chemical properties of their materials, and do not know how to discover, for crucial situations such as a lover's feast, those culinary elements that are almost inflammable and quick to traverse the organic system, like prussic acid, volatile as ether.

A curious thing, but this accord in their opinions about how to live well, this similarity of tastes brought them closely together; this profound understanding of the sensual life, which shone in Samuel's every look and every word, had a strong impact on La Fanfarlo. His phrases, sometimes as brutal as a statistic, sometimes perfumed and delicate as a flower or a sachet, this strange flow of conversation, the secret of which only he knew, ended in his winning the good graces of this charming woman. Moreover, it was not without a sharp and deep sense of satisfaction that he recognized, upon inspecting her bedroom, a perfect congruence of taste and sentiment in the matter of furnishings and interior design. Cramer profoundly hated—and in my view he was absolutely right—those strong right angles in architectural design imported into domestic quarters. The vast chambers of old castles frighten me, and I groan for their inhabitants, forced to make their love in cemetery-like bedrooms, within those huge catafalques they called beds, or on those giant monuments with the pseudonym of chairs. The private rooms of Pompeii were about the size of a hand; the Indian ruins that cover the Malabar coast suggest a similar system. These voluptuous and wise peoples understood the issue perfectly. The intimate feelings can only sound their own depths within a very narrow space.

La Fanfarlo's bedroom was thus very small, very low-ceilinged, stuffed with soft things that were perfumed and dangerous to touch; the air was changed with those bizarre scents that make one want to die there slowly, as if inside a hothouse. The lamplight played on a jumble of lacework and fabrics of a violent yet equivocal coloration. Here and there, on the wall, it lit some paintings marked with a Spanish melodrama: very white flesh against very black backgrounds. And so it was from the depths of this ravishing hovel, at once an evil place and a holy sanctuary, that Samuel saw the new goddess of his heart advancing toward him, in all the radiant and sacred splendor of her nudity.

Where is the man who would not, even at the price of half his earthly days, want to see his dream, his true dream, stand before him without veil, and see his imagination's cherished fantasy let fall, one by one, the garments meant to protect her from the eyes of the vulgar? And yet, see, here is Samuel suddenly seized with a bizarre caprice, setting himself to cry out like an angry child: "I want Columbine, give me Columbine; give her to me exactly as she appeared on the night she drove me mad with her fantastic clothes and her tumbler's bodice!"

La Fanfarlo, surprised at first, was happy to bend to the eccentricity of the man she had chosen, and she rang for Flora; the latter vainly tried to make her understand that it was three in the morning, that everything was locked away in the theater, the concierge sound asleep, the weather dreadful—the storm continued to make its uproar—but one had to obey the woman who was herself obeying, and the maid set off; when Cramer, seized with a new idea, rang the bell and called out in a thundering voice: "And don't forget the rouge!"

This characteristic trait, recounted by La Fanfarlo herself on an evening when her friends were asking about the origins of her affair with Samuel, did not surprise me at all; I recognized the author of *Ospreys* perfectly in all this. He would always love rouge, and the turquoises and the whites, the tinsel of every sort. He would have happily repainted the trees and the sky, and if God had confided nature's plan to him, he would probably have wrecked it.

Samuel's was a depraved imagination, and perhaps for that very reason love was for him less a sensual affair than a rational one. This was above all an admiration of, and an appetite for, the beautiful; he considered reproduction as a vice of love, pregnancy as a spider's trap. He wrote somewhere: "The angels are hermaphrodites, and sterile."—He loved a human body as if it were a harmony of the material, like a fine piece of architecture capable of movement; and this absolute materialism was not so far from the purest idealism. But, with the beautiful, which is the cause of love, there were, he held, two elements: the line and the lure—and important as the line was, the lure for him, on this night anyway, was rouge.

La Fanfarlo thus represented for him both the line and the lure; and when, sitting on the edge of the bed in the careless and victorious calm of the beloved woman, with her hands poised delicately upon him, he gazed at her, he seemed to see infinity behind the beauty's clear eyes, and his own eyes seemed to glide over immense horizons. And, as often is the case with exceptional men, he was often alone in his paradise, no one else being capable of living there with him; and if by chance he tried by force to pull someone else in, she always remained a little behind him; and from within the heaven over which he reigned alone, his love began to turn sad and to suffer from the melancholy of the blue sky, like a lonely king.

But he was never bored with her; and never, when he left his lover's hideaway, tramping heavily along a sidewalk in the morning's coolness, did he experience that egoistic joy signaled by the cigar and the hands in the pockets—which is described somewhere by our great modern novelist.[23]

Instead of heart, Samuel had a noble intelligence, and instead of ingratitude, his enjoyment had engendered a delicious contentment within him, a kind of sensual reverie, which is perhaps a finer thing than love itself, as ordinary people understand it. For her part, La Fanfarlo did her best, spending her most expert caresses on him, for she had understood that this man was worth the effort. She acclimated herself to his language, mystical yet checkered with impurities and the worst crudities.—This all had for her at least the attraction of novelty.

The dancer's falling in love had its visible effects. Some shows had been canceled; she neglected some of her rehearsals; many men envied Samuel.

One night when either chance, Monsieur de Cosmelly's boredom, or a complex set of ruses on the part of his wife had brought the two together at the fireside—after one of those long silences that occur in households where people have nothing to say to each other and a great deal to hide—after having served him the best tea in the

---

23. *The author of "The Girl with the Golden Eyes."* [Baudelaire's note.] Balzac's 1833 novella, *La Fille aux yeux d'or,* can be seen as having influenced Baudelaire's story.

world in a modest, cracked old teapot, perhaps the one dating back to her aunt's chateau—after having sung to him at the piano several bits of music that were in vogue ten years earlier—she said to him, in the sweet and prudent voice of a virtue desirous of making itself amiable, and fearful of antagonizing the object of its affections— that she had felt very sorry for him, that she had wept a great deal, more for him than for herself; that she, in her submissive and entirely devoted resignation, hoped at least that he would find else- where the love that he no longer asked of his wife; that she had suf- fered even more to see him betrayed than to find herself abandoned; that in any case it was in many ways her own fault, that she had forgotten the duties of a loving spouse in failing to warn her hus- band of the danger he was in; that, now, she was quite ready to heal this bleeding wound, and to take entirely upon herself the blame for the imprudence the two had committed, etc.—and all that honeyed words could imply from a scheme authorized by love. She wept, and did it very well; the fire lit up her tears and her face, beautified by sorrow.

Monsieur de Cosmelly said not a word and left. Men who find themselves caught in the trap of their own errors do not much like making their remorse into an offering for clemency. If he went to La Fanfarlo's place, he no doubt discovered the remains of disorder, cigar stubs, and newspapers.

One morning, Samuel was awakened by the insolent voice of La Fanfarlo; he slowly raised his weary head from the pillow where she too reposed, to read a letter that she handed to him:

"Thank you, Monsieur, a thousand thanks; my happiness and my gratitude will be laid to your account in a better world. I accept this. I am taking my husband back, from your hands, and I am taking him with me tonight to our estate at C—, where I will recover both my health and the life I owe to you. Accept, Monsieur, my promise of an eternal friendship. I have always thought so highly of you that I know you would prefer such a friendship to any other sort of rec- ompense."

Samuel, sprawled across the lacy coverlet, and leaning against one of the coolest and loveliest shoulders imaginable, sensed vaguely that he had been had, and began, with some difficulty, to reassemble in his memory the elements of the plot that he had brought to its denouement; but he murmured calmly, "Are our passions really sincere? Who can know with certainty what it is that he wants, and accurately read the barometer of his own heart?"

"What are you saying? What is it you have there? Let me see it," said La Fanfarlo.

"Oh, nothing," said Samuel. "Just a letter from a respectable woman, someone to whom I promised that I would make you my lover."

"You'll pay for that," she said with a forced smile.

It is probably true that La Fanfarlo loved Samuel, but with a love unknown to many hearts, a love with a bitterness in its depths. As for him, his punishment fit his crime. He had often aped passion; he had been forced to undergo it; but this was not the tranquil, calm, strong love inspired by respectable girls, but rather a terrible love, desolating and shameful, the sickly love of courtesans. Samuel had come to know all the tortures of jealousy, and the debased sadness into which we are thrown by an incurable, constitutional disease—in short, all the horrors of that vicious marriage we call concubinage.—As for her, she thrived and fattened daily; she has become a stout beauty, glossy and wily, looking like a sort of ministerial streetwalker. One of these days, she will be fasting for Lent, and distributing alms to her parish. And then, perhaps, Samuel, scarcely dead, will be nailed in his box, as he used to say in better days, and La Fanfarlo, with her nun-like airs, will turn the head of some young heir.—In the meantime, she learns how to produce children; she happily gives birth to a pair of twins.—Samuel fathered four scientific books: one on the four evangelists —another on color symbolism—one on a new system of advertising—and a fourth whose title I don't even want to remember. The frightening thing about this last one is that it had a great deal of verve and energy, and many curiosities. Samuel had the nerve to put as its epigraph, "*Auri sacra fames*"!24—La Fanfarlo wants her

---

24. "The accursed lust for gold" (Virgil, *Aeneid* 3.57). Virgil's word "sacra" meant "cursed," but the word shifted meaning later in history, and by the modern age the phrase could also be translated "the holy lust for gold."

lover to be elected to the Institute, and she schemes to persuade the Ministry to award him the cross of honor.

The poor poet of *Ospreys*! Poor Manuela de Monteverde!—He has fallen low enough.—I recently heard that he founded a socialist paper and that he wants to get into politics.—An indecent mind! as the decent Monsieur Nisard says.[25]

---

25. Désiré Nisard (1806–1888), a much honored literary critic who stood for what he considered the firm morality of classicism and against literary decadence; he considered the seventeenth-century court preacher Jacques-Bénigne Bossuet (1627–1704) to have been the last great French author, and despised Romanticism for its immoral influences.